SPECTRUM

Writing

Grade 4

SPECTRUM

Columbus, Ohio

Credits:
School Specialty Publishing Editorial/Art & Design Team
Vincent F. Douglas, *President*
Tracey E. Dils, *Publisher*
Jennifer Blashkiw Pawley, *Project Editor*
Suzanne M. Diehm, *Project Editor*
Rose Audette, *Art Director*

Contributors:
Mary Waugh
Susan Lowe Wilke
Dr. Betty Jane Wagner
Jan Kennedy
Virginia Allison

Also Thanks to:
Illustrated Alaskan Moose Inc., *Cover Illustration*
4ward Communications, *Interior Design and Production*
Seitu Hayden, *Interior Illustration*

Send all inquiries to:
School Specialty Publishing
8720 Orion Place
Columbus, OH 43240-2111

ISBN 1-57768-914-3

8 9 10 11 12 13 POH 11 10 09 08 07 06

Table of Contents

Table of Contents

Things to Remember About Writing

Prewriting
- Brainstorm topics you might like to write about.
- Create a list of things you could write about each topic.
- Choose the topic you know the most about and that would be of interest to others.
- Collect information.

Writing
- Use sentences in a paragraph only if they tell about the main idea of the paragraph.
- Write directions for doing something in proper order.
- Remember to use sequence words like *first*, *next*, and *last* to put events in the proper order.
- Use *er* or *est*, *more* or *most* to compare things.
- Use details to tell how something looks, sounds, smells, tastes, or feels.
- Think about your purpose before you start writing.
- Write a rough draft focusing on what you want to say rather than the spelling, punctuation, and grammar. You will have the opportunity to make corrections later.

Revising
- Read your rough draft, making changes for interest and clarity.
- Use words that are exact to make your sentences clear.
- Be sure every sentence has a subject and a verb.
- Combine sentences to make your writing smoother.
- Make all verbs in a paragraph or story tell about the same time (verb tense).
- Ask a parent or friend to read your writing and offer suggestions for improvement.

Proofreading
Check to see that:
- you used capital letters correctly.
- you put in correct punctuation marks.
- you used proper grammar.
- all words are spelled correctly.
- you used correct verb forms.

Proofreading Checklist

Use this checklist when proofreading your writing. It will help you remember things you may forget as you review your work.

- [ ] Does each sentence being with a capital letter and end with a period, question mark, or exclamation point?
- [ ] Does each sentence have a subject and verb and a complete thought?
- [ ] Are there any fragments or run-on sentences?
- [ ] Are all words capitalized that should be?
- [ ] Are all words spelled correctly?
- [ ] Have you used troublesome verbs? If so, have you used the correct forms?
- [ ] Does each subject agree with its verb?
- [ ] Did you choose exact words to make your writing clear?
- [ ] Does each pronoun agree with the word it refers to?
- [ ] Have you used apostrophes correctly - to show contractions or possessives?
- [ ] Have all necessary commas been correctly inserted?
- [ ] Have you checked the grammar and usage in your writing?
- [ ] Have you indented your paragraphs?

Proofreading Marks

Use these proofreading marks to help you make corrections in your writing. Try to use a colored pencil or pen when you proofread so that your marks will stand out.

≡	capital letter	Max smith
/	lowercase letter	We like to Eat…
⊙	add period	It was fun⊙
?	add question mark	Do you like pizza?
∧	insert, add this	Ten˄were coming… _people_
✂	delete, take out	Jump all around
∨	add apostrophe	The bike was Sarahs.
¶	new paragraph	happy.¶The boy…
∿	transpose, switch the order	the childsʊ toy
∧	add a comma	hiking, biking˄fishing
⬭	check spelling	I didn't (beleive) her. _believe_

Capitalization
People and Pets

- The word **I** is always capitalized.
  I think it's important to take good care of pets.

- The names of people always begin with a capital letter.
  A pet's name should also be capitalized.
  My cousin **J**ason adopted a dog from the animal shelter.
  The dog is only about ten inches long, but **J**ason named her **T**erminator.

Practice

Read the sentences below. Circle each word that should begin with a capital letter.

I saw a puppy that would make a great pet. His ears stand up like wolves' ears do, so i think we should name him wolf. My older sister colleen is learning to be a veterinarian, and she will help me learn about taking care of a large dog. Since wolf is a malamute, we visited a man who raises these great dogs. A dog named iditarod followed us around. The man, whose name is Jake, explained that iditarod is named for a dogsled race in Alaska. Malamutes are working dogs. We would have to give wolf a lot of exercise, even in very cold weather, and keep him brushed, because malamutes have thick fur. When grown, they can weigh about 85 pounds. jake said that we would have to buy a lot of dog food. We're thinking about that.

Capitalization
People's Titles

- Titles, such as **Mr.**, **Mrs.**, **Miss**, **Ms.**, and **Dr.**, are often included with a person's name. When used as part of someone's name, titles and their abbreviations are always capitalized.

    Dr. Mary Faber talked to our class about first aid.
    Mr. Sherman is the new gym teacher.

- A word that just shows relationship should not be capitalized. Words such as **my**, **your**, **his**, **her**, **its**, **our**, or **their** come before a word that just shows relationship.
    My **g**randfather seems to do everything really well.

However, if a word that shows relationship is used in place of a name, or with a name, it should be capitalized.
    "**G**randfather," I said, "you certainly are a better fisherman than I am."
    "Well," he answered, "**A**unt **M**innow catches more fish than any of us."

Practice

Read the paragraph below. Circle the four words that should be capitalized.

Celia Sandoz grew up in western Nebraska. Her grandfather was Jules Sandoz, a very early settler in the region. Celia's father was also named Jules. Celia had always heard stories about grandfather Jules's family, who had a very difficult life. Celia's aunt, Mari Sandoz, became a famous writer. Once, aunt Mari wrote a book called *Winter Thunder*. It was about Celia's adventure during a rare blizzard in Nebraska. The famous ms. Sandoz also wrote a biography of her father. Travelers today can see the home of mr. Jules Sandoz.

Capitalization
Titles of Written Works

- The important words in the titles of books, stories, poems, songs, movies, and plays should always begin with capital letters. The important words are all words except conjunctions (*and*, *but*, *or*), articles (*a*, *an*, *the*), and prepositions (*on*, *in*, *at*, *of*, *by*).

     Have you read **R**ing of **B**right **W**ater? It's a book about otters.

     The old song "**T**here's a **H**ole in the **B**ucket" is fun to sing.

     We always watch **W**here in the **W**orld Is **C**armen **S**andiego?

- Capitalize an article, conjunction, or preposition if it is the first or last word in a title.

     I saw the play **T**he Wizard of Oz.

     "**A**t the Seaside" is a poem by Robert Louis Stevenson.

     Josh read **A**nd to Think That I Saw It on Mulberry Street to his brother.

Practice

Read each sentence. Circle the capitalization mistake in each title.

1. Artist Marilyn Hafner drew funny pictures for the poem "an Only Child"

   by Mary Ann Hoberman.

2. Tales of A Fourth Grade Nothing is my favorite book by Judy Blume.

3. Did you ever read the book Chicken Soup With Rice by Maurice Sendak?

4. One of Lettie's favorite books is The gold Cadillac by Mildred Taylor.

5. Stephen's choir sang "Swing low, Sweet Chariot" at the winter concert.

6. A good book about stars is The Sky Is Full Of Stars by Franklyn Branley.

7. Casey gave the book Why In the World? to her dad for his birthday.

8. Our class went to see the play The Man Who Loved to laugh.

Capitalization
Places

- Some place-names refer to any one of a group of places, such as streets, cities, countries, continents, islands, oceans, and deserts. These names do not need to be capitalized.

  There are many **m**ountains and **o**ceans in the world.

- Other place-names refer to a specific place. These names should be capitalized.

  The **R**ocky **M**ountains are in **N**orth **A**merica.

  The **H**awaiian **I**slands have a warm climate.

Practice

Read the following paragraph. Circle the seven place-names that should be capitalized. Then write them correctly on the lines below. You may need to use a United States map to help Teresa solve "The Best State" mystery.

On a dusty attic wall, Teresa discovered a faded map. "The Best State" it said on the map. "What's the best state?" Teresa wondered. She read the small print carefully. There were many names on the map. She saw helena and billings. She found flathead lake, clark fork river, and some other rivers and lakes. She found bighorn mountain and then another mountain. To the right of "The Best State" were the words north dakota, and at the top, the word canada. After some investigation, Teresa figured out "The Best State" was _____ .

1. _____

2. _____

3. _____

4. _____

5. _____

6. _____

7. _____

Capitalization
Dates, Holidays, Groups

- The names of specific days, months, and holidays begin with a capital letter.

  I believe that **M**ay will always be my favorite month.
  I love the way our city celebrates **M**emorial **D**ay!
  It's best when a holiday comes on a **M**onday.

- The names of specific organizations and events should also be capitalized.

  The **G**irl **S**couts and **B**oy **S**couts march in the parade every year.
  That weekend our town holds the exciting **L**incolnville **M**usic **F**estival.

Practice

Read the newspaper report below. Circle the words that should be capitalized.

Atlanta, Georgia, welcomed ten thousand athletes from all over the world on july 19, 1996. World-class athletes competed in the summer olympic games. The people of Atlanta worked with the international olympic committee to plan a special schedule of events. It was the 100th anniversary of the modern olympic games.

Proofreading Practice:
Capitalization

As you read the stories below, you will notice that some of the words have not been capitalized. Read the sentences carefully. Use the proofreader's mark (≡) to show which letters should be capitalized.

Walt Disney

Walter elias disney was born in 1901 in chicago, where he later studied art. In 1923, he moved to los angeles, california, hoping to become a film director or producer. When he could not find a job, he decided to produce cartoons. Disney's first success was in 1928 when a mickey mouse cartoon was released. He produced many more cartoon series with the addition of characters, such as donald duck, pluto, and goofy. He released many full-length films, such as pinocchio and fantasia. In 1955, disney opened his first theme park, disneyland, in anaheim, california. A second theme park, walt disney world, opened near orlando, florida in 1971, after disney died. Have you ever been to either of walt disney's theme parks?

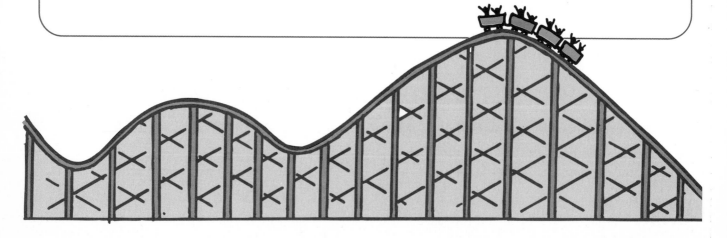

Punctuation
Commas in Series

- Words in a series should be separated by commas.
  The five planets nearest the sun are Mercury, Venus, Earth, Mars, and Jupiter.
  Mars, Earth, and Jupiter have satellites.

Practice

Read the report below. Add commas between the words in a series.

Some modern structures are best known for their great size. The tallest dams in the United States are in Colorado Arizona Idaho and Nevada. The dams in the United States that hold the most water are in Arizona Montana and South Dakota. The United States also has three of the world's longest bridges. They are in New York California and Michigan.

There were also huge structures in the ancient world. Among these were statues gardens sphinxes and temples. Not all of these are still standing, but you still can see the Egyptian pyramids. All of these structures were the results of work by ancient artists architects engineers and laborers.

Punctuation
Commas in Series

- A single sentence can contain a series of people, places, things, or ideas. Use a comma to separate the items in a series.

    Example: The chef is preparing veal, chicken, shrimp, and steak for dinner.

Write an informative sentence containing a series on each line about the topics below. Be sure to use commas to separate the words in a series. The first one is done to help you.

1. Four people in your family
   <u>Kim, Chris, Jon, and Cody are going to see me perform in the school play.</u>

2. Five school subjects

   _____

3. Three U.S. states

   _____

4. Six things to pack for a trip

   _____

5. Four months of the year

   _____

6. Four body organs

   _____

7. Three kinds of math problems

   _____

8. Four medical professionals

   _____

9. Six planets

   _____

10. Five kinds of vegetables

   _____

Punctuation
Commas in Dates and Addresses

- A comma in a date separates the year from other words in the sentence.

    On July 4, 1976, the U.S. celebrated its 200th birthday.

- A comma in an address separates the name of a state from the rest of the sentence.

    The movie was filmed in Cheyenne, Wyoming.

Practice

Read the letter below. Add commas where they are necessary.

72809 East Saddle Road
Omaha NE 68102
October 5 2001

Dear Andrew,

You have to come next month to ride with us in the parade. Afterward, we can go to Council Bluffs Iowa for a picnic. You also said you wanted to see Arbor Lodge. That's in Nebraska City Nebraska, and not far away. We can also go there if you come.

Your friend,

Jenny

Proofreading Practice:
Commas

As you read the story below, you will notice that some commas are missing. Read the sentences carefully. Use the proofreader's mark (∧) to show where commas need to be added.

The Anderson's Family Trip

It was June 2 2002. Andy Anderson was building model airplanes in his attic. His sister Allison his mom and his dad were downstairs packing for the family's cruise to Alaska. They were to leave the next morning. They carefully packed the aspirin army blankets aquatic flippers antiseptics and almanac that they would need for their trip.

The next day, when their car, an Acura, was all packed, the Andersons drove to Arizona to catch a plane to California. This is where they would board the cruise ship, U.S.S. *Alaskan*, to begin their journey. Three hours later, Allison noticed that they had forgotten to bring one last item — Andy! He was home alone, still in the attic with his airplanes! Meanwhile, Andy embarked on his own adventure— home alone, at last!

Proofreading Practice:
Commas

As you read the article below, you will notice that some commas are missing. Read the sentences carefully. Use the proofreader's mark (⋀) to show where commas need to be added.

Soccer

Soccer is probably the world's most popular team sport. It is the national sport of several South American Asian and European countries. The popularity of soccer has grown in the United States in recent years.

In Great Britain, soccer is called football or association football. The word soccer comes from assoc., which is an abbreviation for association.

Each team has eleven players. These players each play a certain position. Some are defenders, and others are forwards and midfielders. The goalkeeper defends the goal and is the only player who is allowed to touch the ball with his hands. All other players may use only their head or body to kick hit or stop the ball.

Possessives
Singular and Plural

- The possessive of a singular noun is formed by adding an apostrophe and **-s**.

    Elena**'s** hat   Cass**'s** jeans

- The possessive of a plural noun that ends in **s** is formed by adding only an apostrophe.

    the teams**'** caps   the players**'** awards

- The possessive of a plural noun that does not end in s is formed by adding an apostrophe and **-s**.

    children**'s** clothing   men**'s** jackets

- The possessive of a hyphenated noun is formed by adding an apostrophe and **-s** to the last word.

    his brother-in-law**'s** jacket

Practice

Write the correct possessive form above each underlined word.

Liz thought it would be cool to visit the past. She thought her <u>great-grandmothers</u>

quilt was beautiful. She wondered how hard the <u>women</u> work was if they had

to take time to make quilts. Did a farm <u>familys</u> day begin early? Were the <u>children'</u>

chores hard? Would she ever know her ancestors' stories?

Proofreading Practice:
Possessives

As you read the article below, you will notice that apostrophes have not been added to show possessives. Read the sentences carefully. Use the proofreader's mark (⋁) to show where apostrophes need to be added. For extra practice use proofreader's marks to correct the errors in capitalization and punctuation that also appear.

Benjamin Franklin

Benjamin franklin was one of americas most famous citizens. He ran a print shop in philadelphia, where he published a newspaper, the pennsylvania gazette, and poor richards almanac. The almanac contained bens wise sayings, such as "a penny saved is a penny earned." He also organized public institutions, such as the first subscription library and americas first city hospital. As a scientist, he demonstrated that lightning is actually electricity. As an inventor, franklin gave us bifocal lenses for glasses the lightning rod and the franklin stove. As a statesman, franklin helped write the declaration of independence and served as minister to france. Ben died in 1790, at the age of 84.

Contractions

- A contraction is a shorter way to say and to spell two words. When you write, you use an apostrophe to show where you have left out a letter.

> The computer store **was not** open that evening.
>
> The computer store **wasn't** open that evening.
>
> **You are** learning to use your computer.
>
> **You're** learning to use your computer.

- In questions, the order of words may be changed when a contraction is used.

> **Can** you **not** understand why we need a computer?
>
> **Can't** you understand why we need a computer?
>
> Why **did** she **not** listen during class?
>
> Why **didn't** she listen during class?

Practice

Look at the underlined words in each sentence. They can be combined to form contractions. Write each contraction on the line at the end of the sentence.

1. The class <u>had</u> <u>not</u> visited Shedd Aquarium before. _____

2. <u>It</u> <u>is</u> home to thousands of beautiful fish. _____

3. <u>Do</u> <u>not</u> tap on the glass. _____

4. <u>That</u> <u>is</u> very disturbing to the fish. _____

5. At the Shedd, <u>there</u> <u>is</u> a giant squid hanging from the ceiling. _____

6. You <u>can</u> <u>not</u> see some of the fish because they hide so well. _____

7. <u>You</u> <u>will</u> want to go to the main aquarium at feeding time. _____

8. A diver will get into the tank; <u>she</u> <u>will</u> feed the fish. _____

9. <u>They</u> <u>are</u> from many different parts of the world. _____

Proofreading Practice:
Contractions

As you read the article below, you will notice that some of the words are italicized. Read the sentences carefully. Rewrite the italicized words as contractions. For extra practice, use proofreaders marks to correct the errors in capitalization and punctuation that also appear.

The History of Basketball

basketball was invented by a man named james naismith he was a physical education teacher at a YMCA school in springfield massachusetts he was told to create an indoor team sport for the winter season naismith asked a janitor to nail two boxes to the gym's balcony opposite each other to be used as goals the janitor however *could not* find boxes, so he nailed up peach baskets instead the new sport then became known as basketball

the first official basketball game *was not* played until january of 1892 it was played with a soccer ball each team had nine players the game was slow-moving because each time a basket was made, someone had to climb a ladder to retrieve the ball over the years changes came about, such as a bottomless net basket, backboards, a larger ball, and some rule changes basketball gradually became the popular sport it is today

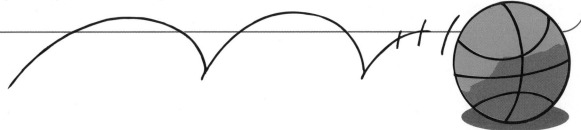

Homophones
Your/You're, Its/It's

- **Your** is a pronoun that shows possession. It always comes before the name of something or someone.
    We saw **your** cousin at the show yesterday.
    Was she wearing **your** hat?

- **You're** is a contraction. It is the shortened form of the two words "you are." The apostrophe means that the letter **a** is missing from **are**.
    You're going to the show tomorrow, aren't you?
    I'll bet **you're** going to be early, as usual!

- **Its** is a pronoun that shows possession. It always comes before the name of something.
    Its mane was huge and made the lion look scary.

- **It's** is a contraction. It is the shortened form of the two words "it is." The apostrophe means that the letter **i** is missing from **is**.
    It's very clear that the lion is dangerous.

Practice

Write **your**, **you're**, **its**, or **it's** in each space in the following report.

If _____ a computer user, you know that when a problem arises with
_____1_____

_____ computer it is called a "bug." _____ a term that was first used
___2___   ___3___

more than fifty years ago when a computer malfunctioned. The programmer found

a dead moth in _____ interior. _____ presence there was probably not
___4___   ___5___

the cause of the problem. If you have a problem with a computer, _____ not
___6___

going to be able to blame moths. _____ probably not _____ fault, either.
___7___   ___8___

Homophones
There/Their/They're, Here/Hear

- **There** may mean "in that place," or it may be used to introduce a sentence before a word such as **was**, **were**, **is**, or **are**. The word **here** is in the word **there**, which may help you remember.

  We found the treasure chest right over **there**.
  There were pieces of gold in the chest.

- **Their** means "belonging to them."
  The pirates said the chest was **their** property.

- **They're** means "they are."
  They're not going to like it if we take their treasure.

- **Here** may mean "in this place," or it may be used to introduce a sentence.
  Let's leave the treasure **here**.
  Here is the map that we used.

- **Hear** means "to listen." The word **ear** is in **hear**, which may help you remember.
  Didn't you **hear** the pirates' warning?

Practice

Read the sentences below. Write **their**, **there**, or **they're** in each space.

Many people work hard to develop _____ muscles. _____ are
                                          1   2
some muscles that you can control. _____ called voluntary muscles.
                                                3
_____ are also involuntary muscles, which you cannot control.
        4

Write **here** or **hear** in each space.

_____ is a fact you may not know. You have about 700 muscles. Would
        5
you like to _____ more information about your muscles?
                    6

Proofreading Practice:
Homophones

As you read the article below, you will notice that some words have been used incorrectly. Read the sentences carefully. Circle the words that are incorrect. Write the correct word above each word that you circled.

Whale or Fish?

The most observable difference between whales and fish is the tail. Fish have vertical tail fins and whales have horizontal tail fins. Their are other differences. Fish breathe through they're gills, while whales breathe through there lungs. Whales can hold their breath for long periods under water. When they need air, they come to the surface and breathe through the blowhole on the top of they're head. A fish lays it's eggs, while a whale gives birth to live young. Whales are warm-blooded. Fish are cold-blooded and a fish's body is covered with scales. A whale has smooth rubbery skin. Whales are also much larger than most fish.

Articles
A, an, and the

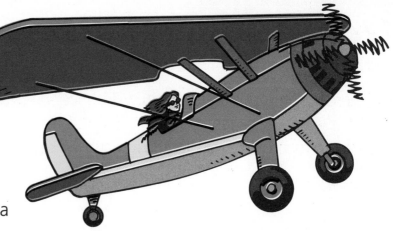

An article is a kind of adjective. There are only three articles: a, an, and the.

- **A** and **an** are indefinite articles because they refer to any one of a group of nouns.

  A small plane and **an** unexpected storm made Beryl Markham's flight dangerous.

- Use the word **a** before words that begin with a consonant sound. Use **an** before words that begin with a vowel sound.

  Markham had been **a** pilot in Africa for many years.

  A compass is **a** useful tool.

  She had flown in **an** open cockpit plane through all kinds of weather.

  She waited **an** hour before taking off.

- **The** is a definite article because it identifies a specific noun.

  Beryl Markham was **the** first person to fly solo across the Atlantic Ocean from east to west.

Practice

Write the correct article **a**, **an**, or **the** in each sentence.

Elephants from Africa are _____ ones with large, fanlike ears. Elephants
1

also live on _____ continent of Asia. _____ elephant has _____
2   3   4

almost hairless body. It also has _____ long, flexible trunk. Elephants are
5

_____ largest mammals that live on land. _____ only larger mammals,
6   7

whales, live in the ocean.

Proofreading Practice:
Articles

As you read the report below, you will notice that some of the articles have been used incorrectly. Read the sentences carefully. Circle the articles that are used incorrectly. Then write the correct article above each word you circled.

Volcanoes

What do Mount Pinatubo in a Philippines, Mount St. Helens in Washington, Kilauea in Hawaii, and Mount Vesuvius in Italy have in common? They are all volcanoes.

Volcanoes are created when magma, which is hot melted rock from inside the earth, is forced upward. It rises through cracks and collects in an magma chamber. Pressure builds until the magma forms an channel through an broken or weakened part of the rock. Then it blasts out a opening called a central vent. Lava, hot gases, and ash spew out onto the land.

Lava is an magma that flows onto a earth's surface. Lava build-ups can form mountains, such as Mount Shasta in California and Mauna Loa in Hawaii.

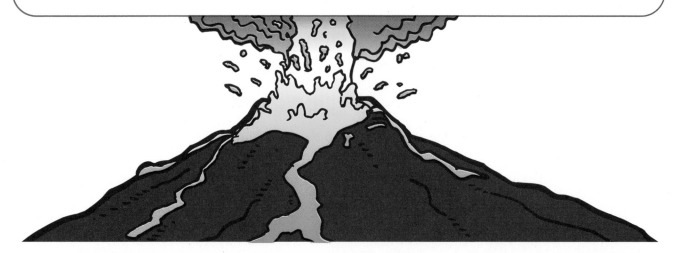

Spectrum Writing Grade 4

Sentence Recognition

A sentence is a group of words which expresses a complete thought.

Look at the group of words below. Write **S** in the blank if the words express a complete thought and **NS** if the words do not express a complete thought.

_____ 1. A greenhouse is a building.

_____ 2. Mostly glass windows and a glass roof.

_____ 3. The lighting in the greenhouse.

_____ 4. The building is not green.

_____ 5. It is colorless.

_____ 6. Many green things in the greenhouse.

_____ 7. The glass protects the plants.

_____ 8. In winter a greenhouse is heated.

_____ 9. Much care is needed for the plants.

_____ 10. Plants are cared for each day.

_____ 11. Bugs are sometimes a problem.

_____ 12. Greenhouse with many different areas.

_____ 13. Spray all plants twice a year.

_____ 14. Plants can be grown during any season.

_____ 15. Many families in the north.

_____ 16. Some vegetables by the door.

_____ 17. You can harvest vegetables in a greenhouse.

_____ 18. When spring comes plants may be removed.

_____ 19. Watch them grow.

Ending Sentences

A sentence needs a good ending. Write an ending to complete each sentence.
  Example: Our teacher is absent today <u>because he is sick</u>.

1. The kids arrived too late for the movie so

   _____

2. Some of the campers began to build a campfire while

   _____

3. The orthodontist wants her to wear braces until

   _____

4. The class arrived early for the museum's exhibit but

   _____

5. Our town is planning to build a new city hall although

   _____

6. The store alarm rang suddenly when

   _____

7. We can meet either at the ticket stand at the game or

   _____

8. Tomorrow our summer vacation is over so

   _____

9. I will bring my music tapes to your house and

   _____

10. The hiker's leader checked his compass while

   _____

Beginning Sentences

A sentence needs a good beginning. Write a beginning to complete each sentence.

  Example: <u>The kids ate pizza</u> and cake at the party.

1. _____ but first

she must finish her homework.

2. _____ so the

mailman left the package by the front door.

3. _____ and put

them away in the closet.

4. _____ or we can

go to a movie instead.

5. _____ while her

brother shoveled snow from the walk.

6. _____ if we

can't find the key to the house.

7. _____ although

the weatherman predicted a sunny day.

8. _____ until it

was time for the plane to take off.

9. _____ because

I was home in bed sick with the flu.

10. _____ so she

ordered a pepperoni pizza instead.

Sentence Identification

- A **statement** tells something or gives information.
  Example: The ball game was delayed because of rain.

- A **question** asks something.
  Example: Would you like to learn to windsurf this summer?

- A **command** tells someone to do something.
  Example: Tell everyone to be ready at five o'clock.

- An **exclamation** shows strong feeling or excitement.
  Example: Look out behind you!

Read each sentence. Write a word from above on each line to name the kind of sentence.

1. _____ Our school is giving a concert next Monday.

2. _____ What time does it begin?

3. _____ Take these tickets to your teacher.

4. _____ We hope to sell five hundred tickets!

5. _____ How many kids are in the orchestra?

6. _____ My brother plays the clarinet.

7. _____ Don't be late for practice.

8. _____ Give the cello to Kim.

9. _____ I want to take violin lessons next year.

10. _____ The band will practice Thursday afternoon.

11. _____ Will you help us set up the stage?

12. _____ Where are the music stands?

13. _____ Don't step on that flute.

14. _____ Raise the curtain.

15. _____ The conductor is ready to begin.

Sentence Punctuation

- A **statement** ends with a period. (**.**)

- A **question** ends with a question mark. (**?**)

- A **command** ends with a period. (**.**)

- An **exclamation** ends with an exclamation point. (**!**)

Read each sentence. Write the correct punctuation in each ☐.

1. Every Saturday morning we help a neighbor ☐

2. Would you like to help us this Saturday ☐

3. Be at my house at 8:00 ☐

4. You can help me gather the supplies we will need ☐

5. I won't be late ☐

6. Today we are raking Mrs. Ray's yard ☐

7. That elm tree is huge ☐

8. Take these lawn bags to Bob and Eric ☐

9. Tell Jan and Pat to mow the back yard ☐

10. Will you help them rake the back yard ☐

11. Don't mow too close to the flowers ☐

12. Look at that big gazebo ☐

13. Mrs. Ray has left lemonade there for us ☐

14. I will mow the front yard ☐

15. Will you sweep the front walks ☐

16. Go ask Mrs. Ray to come see her clean yard ☐

17. She thinks the yard looks super ☐

18. What will we do next Saturday ☐

Writing Sentences

Put a ✔ by each correctly written sentence. Put an **X** by the sentences which contain errors. Rerite the sentences correctly on the lines below.

1. ☐ the evening sky was filled with stars

2. ☐ My committee has agreed to meet next Wednesday.

3. ☐ the tiny mouse ran under the table

4. ☐ all of the runners were exhausted at the finish line

5. ☐ There were thirty kids at Brian's birthday party.

6. ☐ what is your favorite musical instrument

7. ☐ we will be late unless we hurry

8. ☐ do you like to read biographies of famous people

9. ☐ The spectators cheered the winning team.

1. _____

2. _____

3. _____

4. _____

5. _____

6. _____

7. _____

8. _____

9. _____

Spectrum Writing Grade 4

Writing Sentences

Look at the scene below. Write two of each kind of sentence to go with the picture.

Statement

1. _____

2. _____

Question

1. _____

2. _____

Command

1. _____

2. _____

Exclamation

1. _____

2. _____

Describing with Your Senses

Your five senses can give you a lot of information. Imagine that you are walking through a county fair. Think of all the details you would **see**, **hear**, **touch**, **smell**, **taste**.

Even one sense can tell you a lot. Can you recognize someone by just hearing a footstep or a laugh, or smelling a special scent?

Write the name of the sense you would use most to notice each detail listed below. Choose **sight**, **hearing**, **touch**, **smell**, or **taste**. You may list more than one sense for each detail listed. One is done to get you started.

1. tangy orange juice _____ taste _____

2. a porcupine's sharp spines _____

3. puffy clouds _____

4. a creaking door _____

5. a turkey roasting _____

6. a silk shirt _____

7. peppery sausage _____

8. birds chirping _____

Describing with Your Senses

Imagine you are walking inside a deep cave. Your way is lighted by a single candle. Suddenly a drop of water from the roof of the cave puts out the candle. Write five sentences about how you get out of the cave. You'll have mainly your sense of touch to guide you so be sure to include details about touch.

_____

_____

_____

_____

_____

_____

_____

_____

_____

_____

_____

_____

_____

Write On Your Own

Imagine you are a raccoon sniffing around a park. You come across a picnic lunch which is spread out on a blanket on the grass. No one is around. On a separate piece of paper, write five sentences with details describing all the delicious things you smell and taste.

Nouns

- A **noun** is a word that tells who or what did the action or was acted upon by the verb in the sentence.

   The scientists search for the **bones** of **dinosaurs**.
   They use soft **brushes** to remove the **dirt**.

- Nouns can be singular or plural.

   They found a small **bone** next to those large **bones**.

- Some nouns, called proper nouns, name a specific person, place, or thing: *Paul Sereno* and *South America*. They are always capitalized. Nouns like fossils are common nouns. They are capitalized only at the beginning of sentences.

   Paul Sereno found many important fossils in **South America**.

- Proper nouns may be made up of a group of words.

   The **Museum of Natural History** houses dinosaur bones.

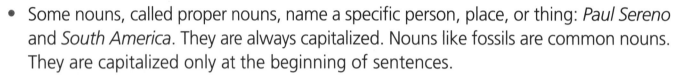

Practice

Find the twenty-nine nouns in the following report. Circle each noun you find. Some nouns are made up of more than one word, like *prairie dogs*.

   The Badlands National Park is in South Dakota. Its rocks, woods, and hills were shaped by wind, rain, frost, and streams. The hills are surrounded by grass. Many animals live there. Visitors can see deer, bison, antelope, coyotes, and prairie dogs. People live in the Badlands, too. Ranchers work on this dry land. Rangers patrol the park. Men and women run stores, hotels, and restaurants.

Spectrum Writing Grade 4

Writing More Exact Nouns

What makes sentences interesting and fun to read? One thing is the words a writer chooses. For example, the sentence below would be more interesting if it had more exact nouns.

The <u>animal</u> played a <u>game</u> with the <u>person</u>.

_____

_____

Rewrite the sentence in two ways on the lines above. Use more exact nouns for each noun that is underlined. Choose from the nouns below or think up your own exact nouns.

Animal: kangaroo, tiger, canary, dolphin
Game: tag, checkers, musical chairs, baseball
Person: rock singer, explorer, princess, dentist

Here are some other nouns. Think of at least three more exact nouns for each. Write them on the lines.

1. Bird: _____ _____ _____

2. Color: _____ _____ _____

3. Flower: _____ _____ _____

4. Sport: _____ _____ _____

5. Vegetable: _____ _____ _____

6. Building: _____ _____ _____

7. Furniture: _____ _____ _____

Writing More Exact Nouns

Choose the more exact noun to complete each sentence
below. Circle the noun you choose.

1. I went into the (building, barn).

2. There were several (horses, animals) inside.

3. I brought a (vegetable, carrot) for each one.

Rewrite the sentences below. Change the nouns that are underlined to more exact nouns.

> The person went into the building to buy vegetables, meat, and fruit. At the checkout counter, the worker gave her only a coin in change. "Things are so expensive," she thought, as an expression crossed her face.

_____

_____

_____

_____

_____

_____

_____

_____

_____

Pronouns

Writers use pronouns to avoid using nouns over and over again.

- A **pronoun** can refer to a person, a place, or a thing. The words *she*, *her*, and *it* are pronouns.

   Franny raced toward **Franny's** goal. Franny knew **the goal** was a mile away.

   Franny raced toward **her** goal. **She** knew **it** was a mile away.

- The form of a pronoun changes depending upon how it is used in the sentence. The pronouns *I*, *myself*, *my*, and *me* all refer to the same person.

   I wanted to hike there by **myself**, but **my** parents wouldn't let **me**.

- Sometimes pronouns make writing confusing. A reader cannot tell if *his* in the first sentence refers to Carl or Jacob. The second sentence makes it clear.

   Carl told Jacob to bring **his** coat.

   Carl said, "Bring **my** coat, Jacob."

Practice

Underline any words that should be changed to pronouns to make the writing smoother and clearer. Write the pronouns above the nouns.

Terri was flying in a hot-air balloon faster than the leader had promised. The wind above the town felt cold. Terri felt uncomfortable and scared. This kind of flying wasn't what the leader had said flying would be, Terri thought. Then another thought came into Terri's mind. The leader hadn't said how Terri could stop flying. Terri remembered a plastic tool in a jeans pocket. Would it help?

Adjectives

- An **adjective** is a word that describes a noun or pronoun. An adjective is a word that can fit in both these blanks:

    The _____ tree is very _____ .

- In the following sentence, the words **smooth**, **dark**, **big**, and **green** are adjectives.

    The artist had **smooth**, **dark** skin and **big**, **green** eyes.

- Adjectives usually come before the words they describe. Sometimes two or more adjectives describe the same word. Adjectives may tell **how many**, **what kind**, or **which one**.

- Adjectives sometimes follow a verb.

    The bicycle was **rusty**.

- Adjectives should be specific. They should help give the reader a clear picture of whatever is being described.

Practice

Circle the twenty-three adjectives in the following paragraph.

The unexpected visitors left their enormous, wooden boats and waded through the rough, warm water to the shore. The visitors were tall and had pale skin. Their dark, long hair was tied back with red, blue, and brown cord. The men's bright clothing covered their bodies. Their wet faces showed that they were tired. The first man to touch shore wore a red cape and a blue hat. He carried a long, black stick, which he pointed at the surprised people standing on the sandy, white shore.

Choosing Exact Adjectives

The sentence doesn't tell you much about Sally's sweater. Is it colorful, well-made, warm, soft? Adjectives like *nice* are not exact. Choosing exact adjectives can help make your meaning clear.

Sally is wearing a nice sweater.

Each sentence that follows gives a choice of two adjectives. Circle the one you think makes the sentence clearer.

1.   That medicine tastes (odd, bitter).

2.   The (bad, vicious) dog bit its owner.

3.   We saw our breath in the (icy, cold) air.

4.   Returning the money was the (good, honest) thing to do.

5.   I like the beach on a (nice, sunny) day.

6.   The figure in the dark cape seemed (mysterious, funny).

7.   The golden, jeweled crown was (pretty, magnificent).

Choosing Exact Adjectives

Instead of repeating the same adjectives in a paragraph, try using **synonyms**. Synonyms are words with almost the same meaning. You probably know many adjectives that are synonyms.

Each word in the first column below has a synonym in the second column. Draw a line to connect the two synonyms.

correct   tiny

awkward   peculiar

lucky   clumsy

little   fortunate

odd   right

Draw a picture of something you like (your bike, computer, a friend, etc.). Write a short description of the picture. Choose exact adjectives to describe the things in the picture.

Expanding Sentences

Expand these sentences by adding all the given adjectives. The first one is done for you.

1. They bought the _____ stove.

   antique   black   rusty

   __They bought the rusty, black, antique stove.__

2. The _____ mailman just rode past.

   whistling   friendly   young

   _____

3. A _____ truck woke the baby.

   garbage   noisy   orange

   _____

4. The Brown's _____ fence is sagging.

   wire   ugly   high

   _____

5. Where is my _____ shirt?

   monogrammed   blue   short-sleeved

   _____

6. They dreamed about a _____ cake.

   sweet   chocolate   luscious

   _____

7. My _____ cap is in the cabin.

   wool   fuzzy   red

   _____

8. Did you find my _____ pen?

   plastic   felt-tipped   red

   _____

9. I would like a pair of _____ boots.

   cowboy   new   brown

   _____

Overused Words

It is easy to use certain words again and again. Try giving these "tired" words a break!
Read each overused word below. Write five synonyms for each word. You may want to
use a thesaurus.

1. wonderful _____ _____ _____ _____ _____

2. beautiful _____ _____ _____ _____ _____

3. good _____ _____ _____ _____ _____

4. okay _____ _____ _____ _____ _____

5. many _____ _____ _____ _____ _____

Read the sentences below. Choose a synonym from your list above to replace each
underlined word. Rewrite the sentences using the new words.

Last Friday our class had a wonderful time at the
Tropical Gardens. We saw many flowers, trees, and
plants. The exotic birds were beautiful. We had a good
guide. He said it was okay to take lots of pictures.

_____

_____

_____

_____

_____

_____

_____

_____

Descriptive Sentences

Turn a good sentence into a great sentence by using more descriptive words.

Example: The couple cut the cake.
                The **newlywed** couple cut the
                five tier wedding cake.

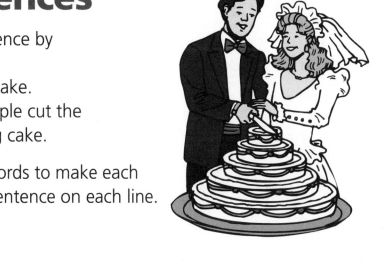

Read each sentence. Add descriptive words to make each a great sentence. Write the improved sentence on each line.

1. The man climbed the mountain.

_____

_____

2. The group found a buried tomb.

_____

_____

3. The girls painted a sign.

_____

_____

4. The sunlight came through the window.

_____

_____

5. Ice cream dripped down the cone.

_____

_____

6. The snake moved down the tree.

_____

_____

7. The storm rocked the boat.

_____

_____

Writing Details from Pictures

Details are small bits of information. Details tell how things look, sound, smell, feel, taste, or seem. Exact details can make a description more interesting.

Read the paragraph below. Underline all the details you find. One has been done to get you started.

It was a <u>dry, hot</u> afternoon. An old, spotted pony came limping slowly down the dirt road. His thick hair was caked with dust. Suddenly, the tired animal stopped in his tracks. He saw a giant maple tree close by. Under the tree was a thick patch of grass. It was the perfect place to eat and rest.

Now put a check mark below the picture of the animal described in the paragraph.

1. _____   2. _____   3. _____

Writing Details from Pictures

List four details you find in the picture above.

1. _____

2. _____

3. _____

4. _____

Now use your list of details to write four sentences about the picture.

1. _____

2. _____

3. _____

4. _____

Write On Your Own

On a separate sheet of paper, write a short description of a room in your home, including details. Then draw a picture of the room, showing each detail you've described.

Adverbs

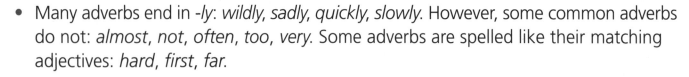

- An **adverb** is a word that describes a verb, an adjective, or another adverb. Adverbs tell *how, when, where,* and *how much*.

    The children giggled **wildly** as the clowns ran past.
        (*Wildly* is an adverb that describes the verb *giggled*.)
    One large clown sat **very** carefully on a tiny stool.
        (*Very* is an adverb that describes the adverb *carefully*.)
    Another clown carried a **brightly** painted banner.
        (*Brightly* is an adverb that describes the adjective *painted*.)

- Many adverbs end in *-ly*: *wildly, sadly, quickly, slowly*. However, some common adverbs do not: *almost, not, often, too, very*. Some adverbs are spelled like their matching adjectives: *hard, first, far*.

Practice

Find the thirteen adverbs in the following paragraph. Circle each adverb you find. Remember, an adverb will tell *how, when, where,* or *how much*.

> The class had studied seriously to learn about the historically important pier. They had finally come to visit it, but it was too crowded to see much. People were packed tightly in the restaurants. The museum was completely filled with visitors. The air-conditioned bookstore felt only slightly cool inside because of the crowds. The lines for the rides were ridiculously long. Why was everybody so happy? Why were they all extremely glad that they had come to this very exciting place?

Writing with Adverbs

We went there then.
We went to the museum on Saturday afternoon.

Which sentence above gives you more information? Words like **there** and **then** are **adverbs**. They tell where and when. Word groups like **to the museum** and **on Saturday afternoon** are **adverbial phrases**. They tell where and when, but they give more exact details.

Here are some other adverbial phrases:

Where	**When**
under the bed	after the game
aboard the ship	before next Tuesday

Replace each underlined adverb below with an adverbial phrase that gives more information. Write your new sentence on the blank line.

1. A mosquito flew <u>somewhere</u>.

_____

2. The bus leaves <u>sometime</u>.

_____

3. Let's go <u>there then</u>.

_____

Writing with Adverbs

Adverbs like **excitedly** tell how. Many adverbs that tell how are formed by adding **ly** to adjectives.

> Lydia talked excitedly about the museum.
> excited + ly = excited<u>ly</u>

Some adverbs are formed by changing the **y** in an adjective to **i**, then adding **ly**.
> clumsy + ly = clumsi<u>ly</u>

Change each adjective below into an adverb that tells how.

1. alert _____

2. cautious _____

3. fortunate _____

4. quick _____

5. angry _____

6. easy _____

Write a few sentences about the museum on the previous page, or a museum you like to visit. Try to use at least two how adverbs, and two when and where adverbial phrases.

_____

_____

_____

_____

_____

_____

Write On Your Own

Think about another place you like to visit. On a separate piece of paper, write five sentences describing this place. Try to use adverbs and adverbial phrases to make your sentences clear and interesting.

Expanding Sentences

You can **s-t-r-e-t-c-h** a sentence by adding more information.

Stretch these sentences by adding words to answer each question.
   Example: The plane landed. When? The plane landed at 1:30 p.m.

1. We are all going to the airport. How?

   _____

2. I am taking three pieces of luggage. Why?

   _____

3. The passengers are lined up. Why?

   _____

4. The baggage was stacked. Where?

   _____

5. She bought, her ticket. How?

   _____

6. We will arrive in Los Angeles. When?

   _____

7. The tourists brought plenty of film. Why?

   _____

8. Our flight attendant is helping us. How?

   _____

9. We will fasten our safety belts. When?

   _____

10. The plane is beginning to move. Where?

   _____

11. A delicious dinner was served. When?

   _____

12. Our cautious pilot avoided the stormy clouds. How?

   _____

Verbs

- A **verb** tells what the person, place, or thing in a sentence is doing, or it links or connects the subject to the rest of the sentence. A verb might tell about being rather than acting. The words *felt* and *hiked* are verbs.

    The boys **felt** tired as they **hiked** on the trail.

- Verbs also show whether something happens in the present, the past, or the future. The word *hike* is present tense, *hiked* is past tense, and *will hike* is future tense.

    Today I **hike**. Yesterday I **hiked**. Tomorrow I **will hike**.

- Verbs must match their subjects. In the present tense, the verb *walk* changes when its subject is a third-person singular noun, such as *girl*.

    I often **walk** on that trail.

    Girls from my school **walk** on it, too.

    I know a girl who **walks** on the trail every day.

- Some verbs express a state of being. The most common verbs that show being are *am*, *is*, *are*, *was*, *were*, and *be*.

    The cougar **was** huge, and the boys **were** terrified.

Practice

Think of a verb to complete each sentence. Remember to use the correct verb form.

> Mountain climbing _____ a popular sport. People _____ mountains
> 　　　　　　　　　　　　1　　　　　　　　　　　　　　　　　　　2
>
> for many reasons. Some people _____ the challenge of trying to reach high
> 　　　　　　　　　　　　　　　　3
>
> and dangerous places. Others _____ to explore the outdoors and _____
> 　　　　　　　　　　　　　　　4　　　　　　　　　　　　　　　　　　5
>
> the beauty of nature. Whatever the reason, mountaineering _____ serious
> 　　　　　　　　　　　　　　　　　　　　　　　　　　　　　6
>
> business. Every climber _____ to work with experienced teachers.
> 　　　　　　　　　　　　7

Subject-Verb Agreement

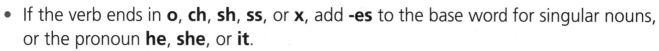

- In the present tense of most verbs, the endings change to match the subject. If the subject is a singular noun or the pronoun **he**, **she**, or **it**, the verb should end in **-s**.

    She **walks** with us.   John **walks** for exercise.
    It **walks** on its hind legs.   He **walks** with a cane.

- If the subject is a plural noun, or the pronoun **I**, **we**, **you**, or **they**, you do not add **-s** to the verb.

    They **walk** often.   I **walk** every day.
    You **walk**, too.   The workers **walk** to the fields.

- If the verb ends in **o**, **ch**, **sh**, **ss**, or **x**, add **-es** to the base word for singular nouns, or the pronoun **he**, **she**, or **it**.

    I **fish**.   Do you **fish**?   Jason **fishes** every day.

Practice

In the spaces below, write the correct forms of the verbs in parentheses.

1. A camel _____ heavy burdens. (carry)

2. Camels _____ in Africa. (live)

3. The camel _____ a little like some of its relatives in America. (look)

4. You _____ what a llama is, don't you? (know)

5. The furry animal _____ a little like a camel. (behave)

6. A llama, though, _____ not have a hump. (do)

7. A llama _____ a burden, just as a camel does. (carry)

8. The animals _____ many pounds at a time. (carry)

9. A herder _____ the valuable animals. (watch)

Subject–Verb Agreement

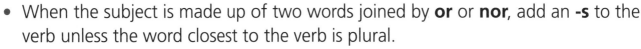

- When the subject of a sentence is one thing or one person, except **you** or **I**, add an **-s** to the verb.
  Alan seems tired in the early morning.

- When the subject of the sentence is made up of two singular persons or things joined by **and**, use a verb that does not end in **-s**.
  Alan and his trainer seem tired when they come in.

- When the subject is made up of two words joined by **or** or **nor**, add an **-s** to the verb unless the word closest to the verb is plural.
  Neither **Alan nor his trainer seems** tired.
  Neither **Alan nor his friends waste** time.

- Take special care when a helping verb comes before its subject, as it does in many questions.
  Why **do skaters and coaches** work so hard?

Practice

Underline the words that make up the subject of each sentence. In the blank, write the correct form of the verb in parentheses.

Why _____ readers and television viewers get animal groups mixed up?
1 (do, does)
Often, the viewer and the reader _____ that animals are alike or
2 (decide, decides)
different because of their appearance. Both the cassowary and the emu

_____ to the group of birds that can't fly. On the other hand, koalas
3 (belongs, belong)
and kangaroos seem different, but they both _____ into the same species.
4 (fit, fits)
However, the bear and the koala are different and _____ their young
5 (raise, raises)
in different ways.

Subject–Verb Agreement

Practice

Write three sentences comparing the two vehicles in the drawing. How are they alike? How are they different?

1. _____

_____

2. _____

_____

3. _____

_____

Practice

Write five sentences about the shepherd in the picture. Describe how he feels about his work. Use at least three of these verbs, adding correct endings: **watch**, **play**, **carry**, **walk**, **climb**.

1. _____

_____

2. _____

_____

3. _____

_____

Verb Tense

- The past tense of a verb tells you that something happened in the past. The past tense of most verbs is formed by adding **-ed**.

   I love to **learn** new songs. I **learned** a funny
   one yesterday.

- The past tense of verbs that end in silent **e** is formed by dropping the **e** and adding **-ed**. If the verb ends with a single consonant, double the consonant and add **-ed**.

   The song was about a cowhand who had to **saddle** a horse.
   After he had **saddled** it, it refused to move.
   The cowhand tried to **plan** ways to make the horse move, but everything
   he **planned** failed.

- The past tense of some verbs is formed by changing the spelling of the verb.

   I like to **sing**. I **sang** the saddle song over and over.
   I **write** stories. I **wrote** a story for the school newspaper.
   I **know** that I **knew** all the words perfectly yesterday.
   I **think** I've forgotten them, but I **thought** I had them memorized.

Practice

Write the correct past tense verb above each underlined verb in the paragraph below.

I <u>think</u> television <u>is</u> unhealthy for kids. We <u>sit</u> around too much. How many
    1   2   3

of us <u>play</u> sports every single day? <u>Are</u> most teens in sports? You say that you
       4   5

<u>skate</u>? You <u>love</u> hiking? Well, most kids <u>walk</u> very short distances! We all <u>plan</u>
  6   7   8   9

to exercise, right? Next week, be able to say, "I <u>exercise</u> every day!"
                                                      10

Verb Tense

Read the sentences below. Then write the past tense form of the verbs given.

1. Julie <u>watches</u> the parade. _____

2. Ted <u>calls</u> his horse. _____

3. He <u>walks</u> quickly. _____

4. They <u>play</u> hard. _____

5. Sheila <u>dances</u> beautifully. _____

Some verbs don't add **-d** or **-ed** to form their past tense. Instead they change spelling. For example: **fly — flew, take — took, drink — drank**. If you are not sure of how the past tense of a verb is spelled, look it up in your dictionary.

Read the sentences below. Then write the past tense form for each verb given.

1. Coreen <u>drinks</u> lots of fruit punch. _____

2. Robert <u>flies</u> his model airplane. _____

3. Barbara <u>leaves</u> early in the day. _____

4. Jason <u>runs</u> fast. _____

5. We <u>go</u> to a basketball game. _____

Practice

Use the past tense of **watch**, **run**, and **fly** in three sentences of your own.

1. _____

_____

2. _____

_____

3. _____

_____

Proofreading Practice:
Verb Agreement and Tense

As you read the story below, you will notice that some of the verbs are not used correctly. Read the sentences carefully. Circle the verbs that are incorrect. Write the verbs correctly making sure that the verbs you write are correct in agreement and tense.

Young George Washington

George was born on February 22, 1732 in Virginia. His family move to an undeveloped plantation, later called Mount Vernon, when he were three years old. They had no nearby neighbors.

George didn't receive many years of formal education. He wrote his lessons on sheets of paper that his mother then sewed into a notebook. His favorite subject were math. His father had plan to send him to school in England, but when George were just eleven years old, his father died. George was then needed by his mother on the farm. At a young age, George helped manage a plantation worked by twenty slaves. No one know for sure if he really chopped down his father's cherry tree, but he were a quiet, patient, dependable, and honest young man.

Writing with Interesting Verbs

Look at the picture and read the sentence below.

Harry **went** up to the hurdle and **jumped** over it.

The underlined words in the sentence are verbs. Verbs express action. The verbs *went* and *jumped* tell something about what is happening in the picture. But these verbs could be more interesting. Read the next sentence that uses more interesting verbs to tell about the picture.

Harry **raced** up to the hurdle and **leaped** over it.

Read the following list of verbs. Then write two more interesting verbs for each one given. One is done to get you started. If you need help, use a dictionary.

1. look   _____peek_____   _____glance_____

2. talked   _____   _____

3. ate   _____   _____

4. walked   _____   _____

5. went   _____   _____

6. touched   _____   _____

Writing with Interesting Verbs

All of the verbs are underlined in the sentences below. Using more interesting verbs, rewrite the sentences on the lines below. Use some of the interesting verbs that you wrote on the previous page or think up other interesting verbs.

> Sam Spade <u>went</u> to the scene of the crime. He <u>looked</u> around for clues. Then he <u>walked</u> back to his office. He <u>ate</u> a sandwich quickly while he <u>moved</u> back and forth in the room. After a while, he <u>touched</u> his desk with his foot. He decided that his pet Chihuahua had <u>taken</u> his hat after all.

Write On Your Own

On separate sheet of paper, write five sentences about one of your hobbies. Use interesting verbs; share your writing with a friend.

Proofreading Practice:
Writing with Interesting Verbs

As you read the story below, you will notice that some of the verbs are italicized.
Read the sentences carefully. Write a more interesting verb above each italicized verb.

Gentlemen: Start Your Engines

I'll be the first ten-year-old in history to *be* in the Indy 500. I can hear it now.
Reporters will grab their microphones to inform the world of the amazing event.
"Young Zach Rossfield is in Indianapolis to *run* his car, an Iola 650, after qualifying
in the time trials with a speed of 221.6 miles per hour.

Zach's red-and-greystriped beauty was *made* by his dad and grandpa back
home in Columbus, Ohio. There was no scrimping on this racer. Krazy Kid Motor
Oil, Zach's sponsor, paid all expenses including Goodyear racing radials. When
interviewed today, Zach *said* that he feels a little nervous about the race but plans
to go home with part of the $7 million purse. He promised to keep a cool head
and try his best to drive safely.

"Zach! Zach! Earth to Zach!" my friend Henry yelled, breaking me out of the
best daydream I've had in ages.

"Huh?" I mumbled.

Henry *said* impatiently, "I asked if you'd
like to race our go-carts after school."

Proofreading Practice:
Writing with Interesting Verbs

As you read the story below, you will notice that some of the words are italicized. Read the sentences carefully. Using the Word List, choose a better, more interesting word for each italicized word you find.

Word List

enormous	gazing	peered	shivery	spectacular
rush	wailing	eagerly	clever	amazed

Thanksgiving Day Parade

It was a *cold* Thursday in November in New York City. Thomas *looked* out the window of his New York City condo overlooking Central Park. People were crowded on every street corner and lined every sidewalk. *Excitedly* looking in the direction of the approaching floats were scores of children. Thomas heard bands playing, sirens *going*, and voices singing. What was happening here? Then Thomas followed the stares of the people *looking* up, up, up. He was *surprised* to see *huge* helium balloons of every color, size, and shape. He wanted so badly to *hurry* out of his condo to see more of this *neat* event, but he knew he couldn't. Thomas would never be able to find his way through the crowds and make it home in time for dinner–unless he devised a very *smart* plan.

Spectrum Writing Grade 4

Adjectives that Compare

- Most adjectives can be compared by adding **-er** to compare two things, and **-est** to compare more than two.

  Hyenas are **fast** runners. Gazelles are **faster** than hyenas.
  Cheetahs are the **fastest** of all.
  A hippopotamus is a very **large** mammal, but an elephant
  is **larger**. The **largest** of all is the whale.

- Some adjectives are compared by placing the word **more** or **most** in front of the adjective.

  Deer are **frequent** visitors to our camp, but black bears are **more**
  frequent than the deer. The **most frequent** visitors are raccoons.

- To compare some adjectives, change the word completely.

  Our back porch is a **good** place to watch deer.
  The park at the edge of town is **better** than the porch.
  The **best** of all places is the beach on Summer Lake.
  The mosquitoes are **bad** this year.
  Some people say they were **worse** two years ago.
  Everyone agrees the **worst** year was 1990.

Practice

Write the correct form for each adjective shown in parentheses.

1. This path is _____ than that one. (safe)

2. This is the _____ view in the park. (good)

3. Would you be _____ on a raft than in a canoe? (comfortable)

4. Upsetting the canoe was the _____ accident I ever had! (scary)

5. Ms. Jason was _____ than I was. (helpful)

Adjectives that Compare

Practice

Using the picture below, write a sentence using a comparative form of each word in parentheses.

1. (tall) _____

_____

2. (silly) _____

_____

3. (wise) _____

_____

4. (good) _____

_____

Comparing Two Things

The suitcase on the left is **lighter**.
The suitcase on the right must be **fuller**.

- The sentences above are **comparisons**.
  Comparisons tell how things are alike or different.

- Comparisons often use **adjectives**. Read the underlined adjectives in the sentences above. What two letters do they end in? When two things are compared, the ending **er** is added to many adjectives.

Look at the pairs of pictures that follow. For each pair, write a sentence comparing the two things. Use the *er* form of the adjective given.

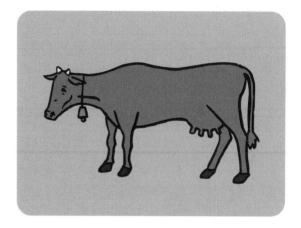

1. fat: _____

2. clean: _____

Comparing Two Things

- With longer adjectives, we use the word **more** to make comparisons: **more delicious**, **more beautiful**.

Finish each comparison below. Use words from the Word List, or think of your own adjectives. Use each adjective only once.

Word List

more expensive	faster	brighter
more playful	deeper	bigger

1. An apartment house is _____ than a cottage.

2. A kitten is _____ than a cat.

3. A car is _____ than a bicycle.

4. A lake is _____ than a puddle.

5. The sun is _____ than the moon.

Write On Your Own

Choose one of the pairs below to compare. Make a list of -er adjectives for each one in the pair. Then, on a separate sheet of paper, write three sentences, using the adjectives to compare the two things.

Sunday and Monday   a dog and a cat

a peach and a lemon   you and a friend

Comparing More Than Two Things

Brenda is the **most skillful** skier on this hill.
She reached the bottom in the **fastest** time.

Read the sentences above. They compare Brenda to some other people. The adjectives used in the sentences are the words **fastest** and **most skillful**. When we compare more than two things, we add the ending **est** or use the word **most** with the adjective.

Write a sentence that uses each adjective below. Look at the picture of the skiers to give you some ideas.

1. coldest: _____

_____

2. most awkward: _____

_____

3. most difficult: _____

_____

Comparing More Than Two Things

Look at the three winners of the Centerville Dog Show. Write three or four sentences comparing the three. Use at least one adjective in each sentence. Here are some adjectives you may wish to use: **smallest**, **furriest**, **biggest**, **longest**, **most playful**.

_____

_____

_____

_____

_____

_____

_____

_____

Write On Your Own

Books of records often list the "most" and the "best." On a separate sheet of paper, make up your own list of at least six records. List things or people you think are the most or the best. Tell why you chose each one. Here are some ideas to get you started.

Most delicious food   Most unusual hobby

Funniest person   Most useless object

Writing Comparisons Correctly

- You add **est** or **most** to an adjective when you compare more than two things. But how do you know which to add? With one-syllable adjectives and many two-syllable   adjectives, use *est*:

  dull, dull**est**   happy, happi**est**

- Use **most** with long adjectives. Also use **most** with adjectives that end in **ful**, **ous**, **al**, and **ish**:

  fortunate, **most** fortunate   careful, **most** careful

Read the paragraph below. In each sentence there is a choice of words in parentheses. Underline the correct form.

> This part of the jungle was the (interestingest, most interesting). Snakes hung
>
> from the (lowest, most low) branches of the trees. Then we saw the (magnificentest,
>
> most magnificent) building we had ever seen. Surely this was the Temple of Bom
>
> Gabala, the (mysteriousest, most mysterious) temple in the world.

Writing Comparisons Correctly

Remember to use **er** or **more** to compare two items. Use **est** or **most** to compare more than two things. Each label below contains two choices. Underline the word which correctly describes the pictured item.

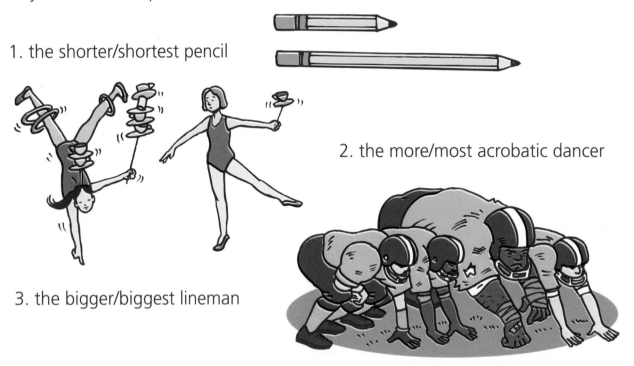

1. the shorter/shortest pencil

2. the more/most acrobatic dancer

3. the bigger/biggest lineman

Some adjectives have special forms: **good, better, best**   **bad, worse, worst**

Write the correct form of each word in parentheses.

1. Arnie is a (good) _____ player than I am.

2. In fact, he is the (good) _____ player on the team.

3. Your yard looks (bad) _____ since you stopped mowing the lawn.

4. It is the (bad) _____ looking yard on the block.

Write On Your Own

Write the following adjectives on a separate piece of paper: **noisy, comfortable, good, delicious, funny**. For each, write a pair of comparison sentences. In one sentence, compare two things. In the other, compare more than two things. Be sure to write the adjective forms correctly.

Writing Comparisons with <u>like</u> and <u>as</u>

Comparing Dad to a firecracker gives a clearer and more interesting picture than just saying he's angry. A comparison that uses the word **like** or **as** is called a **simile**. Similes can help make writing clearer and more lively.

Read these similes and answer the questions.

a. My stomach feels as empty as a doughnut hole.

b. The stage was as bright as a million fireflies.

1. In simile a, the two things being compared are

_____ and _____

2. In simile b, the two things being compared are

_____ and _____

Writing Comparisons with <u>like</u> and <u>as</u>

Now try writing some similes of your own.
Complete the sentences below with the most
expressive comparisons you can think of.

1. At the sound of the starting gun, Elena ran as fast as

_____

2. When I shined Pa's old boots, they gleamed like

_____

3. The superjet stood on the runway, huge and shiny like

_____   _____

_____   _____

• You can describe something with several similes, making a simile poem.

  Complete this simile poem.

   My striped scarf is as colorful as a field of tulips.

   Its wool feels soft, like _____ _____

   It keeps me as warm as _____ _____

   When I wear it, I look like _____ _____

Write On Your Own

On a separate sheet of paper, write your own simile poem. Choose something you own
or something you see every day. Describe the object, using three or more similes, and
see how unusual and interesting this everyday object becomes. Here are some things you
might describe: a pet, a bike, a tree, a building.

Spectrum Writing Grade 4

Writing Similes

A simile is a comparison of two things using **like** or **as**.

The similes below have been used too often. Make a new comparison.

OLD

1. as red as a beet
2. as fresh as a daisy
3. as black as coal
4. as wise as an owl
5. as cold as ice
6. as strong as an ox
7. to swim like a fish
8. to grow like a weed
9. as slow as a turtle
10. as hungry as a bear
11. to run like the wind
12. as white as snow
13. as big as a house
14. to sleep like a baby
15. as round as a ball

NEW

1. as red as _____
2. as fresh as _____
3. as black as _____
4. as wise as _____
5. as cold as _____
6. as strong as _____
7. to swim like _____
8. to grow like _____
9. as slow as _____
10. as hungry as _____
11. to run like_____
12. as white as _____
13. as big as _____
14. to sleep like _____
15. as round as _____

Choose 5 of your new similes and use them in a sentence.

1. _____
2. _____
3. _____
4. _____
5. _____

Figures of Speech

- **Figures of speech** can make sentences more interesting.
  Here are four popular kinds of figures of speech:

  Personification — gives human characteristics to things.
    Example: The sun touched us with its warm fingers.

  Hyperbole — a great exaggeration.
    Example: She's the happiest person in the universe.

  Simile — compares two unlike things, using **like** or **as**.
    Example: He is hungry as a horse.

  Metaphor — only suggests a comparison of two unlike things.
    Example: The vacant field was a desert.

Read each sentence. Underline the figure of speech. Write the name of the figure of speech on each line.

_____ 1. The wind howled as the storm grew closer.

_____ 2. The little lady nibbled at her lunch like a bird.

_____ 3. Sarah's little sister was a doll in her new clothes.

_____ 4. The camp leader said he would never sleep again.

_____ 5. The banana cream pie was heaven.

_____ 6. We were as busy as bees all day long.

_____ 7. His patience just flew out the window.

_____ 8. He said that his life was an open book.

_____ 9. The newlyweds were as happy as two lovebirds.

_____ 10. The heavy fog crept slowly to shore.

_____ 11. The champion wrestler is as strong as an ox.

_____ 12. The twins were angels for helping their mom.

_____ 13. I am so full that I never want to eat again.

_____ 14. Sometimes my memory is a blank tape.

Rewriting

You already know that **proofreading** means reading over your work and correcting any errors it may have. Along with proofreading your writing, you may often have to rewrite it. Rewriting means improving your writing. You may want to use more exact nouns, verbs, or adjectives. Or you may want to put better rhythm in your writing by changing the length of your sentences. Or you just may want to make your writing clearer.

Read the following paragraph. Then read the "rewrite" of the same paragraph below. Finally write answers to the questions that follow.

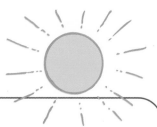

It was a good day. The sun was out. The air was nice. The trees moved in the wind. I felt very nice.

Saturday was a delicious fall day. The sun was bright, and the air was crisp and clear. The trees rustled leaf-songs. I felt as excited as the flaming colors of red, yellow, and orange.

1. What is one more exact noun that is used in the rewrite?

   _____

2. What more exact verb is used?

   _____

3. What more exact adjectives are used?

   _____

4. Write the first three words of the two sentences that are combined.

   _____

5. Do you think the rewrite is an improvement? _____
   Why? _____

Polishing Your Writing

Do your own rewrite of the next paragraph on the lines below. Look back at the rewrite on the previous page if you need help.

> She got up one morning. She got dressed. She had breakfast. She went outside. She played all afternoon.

_____

_____

_____

_____

_____

_____

_____

_____

_____

_____

Writing About a Person

Use some of the words on the left to finish the character descriptions. You may also choose your own words.

honest

fearless

handsome

stubborn

graceful

depressed

gloomy

lazy

happy-go-lucky

sensible

cowardly

smiling

red-headed

tall

blonde

full mouth

turned-up nose

button nose

gray eyes

long-legged

wide shoulders

erect posture

curly hair

messy hair

tiny mouth

a four-year-old boy:
Brad is very active and eager to play. His body is very wiry.

_____

_____

_____

_____

_____

a ten-year-old girl:
Nancy has lovely brown curly hair and sparkling blue eyes.

She has a _____ nose and

_____ mouth. Her actions

_____

_____

_____

a teenager:
This teenager is thoughtful, capable and nice to know. He

_____

_____

_____

_____

_____

Finding the Main Idea

Look at the picture.

Underline the sentence below that tells what the whole picture is all about.

1. The piano player is holding her ears.

2. No one likes the man's singing.

3. There are tomatoes on the stage.

The sentence that tells what the whole picture is all about is called the **main idea**. The other sentences describe **details** in the picture. One detail of the picture is the woman holding her ears. Write another detail of the picture.

_____

_____

Paragraphs also have main ideas and details. A paragraph is a group of detail sentences that tell about one main idea.

Finding the Main Idea

Read the paragraph below. Pay attention to the detail sentences.

> Marie pushed her carrots to one side of her plate. She flattened the top of her mashed potatoes and placed one carrot there. Then she cut her meat into small pieces. She put them in a circle around the mound of potatoes. "Aren't you going to eat, Marie?" her mother asked.

Now underline the sentence below that tells the main idea.

1. Marie pushed her carrots aside.

2. Marie's mother asked her a question.

3. Marie played with her food instead of eating it.

Read the next paragraph. Write two details from it. Then write its main idea.

> What a day Mr. Montez had! First the car wouldn't start. Then he found two angry customers waiting for him at the store. About noon, he got a headache that lasted all afternoon. That night, his favorite TV show was replaced by a special on turnips.

Detail: _____

Detail: _____

Main Idea: _____

Writing a Topic Sentence

Sometimes the main idea of a paragraph is stated in one sentence in the paragraph. This sentence is called the **topic sentence**. Topic sentence is another name for the main idea.

Read the paragraph below. Think about the main idea.

> She was the prettiest horse I ever saw. Her hide shone like a polished copper kettle. Her tail streamed in the breeze when she trotted, and she tossed her head proudly.

1. Draw a line under the topic sentence.
2. Write two details.

_____

_____

The topic sentence often comes at the beginning of a paragraph. But sometimes it comes at the end or even in the middle.

Read the paragraph and the one on the next page. Underline the topic sentence in each.

> Julio started down the stairs. He was careful not to walk on loose steps that might groan under his weight. His hand gripped the rail, but not too tightly. What if it creaked? Holding his breath, he tiptoed from step to step. Finally he stood in the dark at the bottom. Julio got to the basement without making a sound.

Writing a Topic Sentence

My sister doesn't like the rain. But I think rainy days can be fun. We play card games for hours, and I usually win. We dress up in old hats and capes and pretend we're old-fashioned ladies. Most of all, I like to sit on the window seat and read while rain splatters on the windowpane outside.

The topic sentence in the next paragraph is missing. Add up the detail sentences to find the main idea. Then write a good topic sentence.

The burning sun rose higher over the city. People leaned out of windows and fanned themselves. Children sat limply on curbs. Ice cream and cold drink sellers were the only people working. _____

_____

Write On Your Own

On another sheet of paper, write your own paragraph. Choose one of the topic sentences below or think of your own. Try putting your topic sentence first. Then rewrite your paragraph, moving your topic sentence to another place in the paragraph.

I love to walk in the park in the spring.

Photos help me to remember good times.

My old sneakers have been good friends.

Topic Sentences

- A paragraph is a group of sentences that tells about one main idea. One of the sentences states the main idea. That sentence is called the **topic sentence**. The topic sentence is usually the first sentence in the paragraph.

    Example: (The topic sentence is underlined.)

    <u>Three planets in our solar system have rings around them.</u> The planets with rings are Saturn, Uranus and Jupiter. The rings are actually thin belts of rocks that orbit the planets. Saturn is the most famous ringed planet.

Underline the topic sentence in the paragraph below.

> Every weekday morning I follow a basic routine to get ready for school. I get up about 7 a.m., wash my face, and get dressed. Then, I eat breakfast and brush my teeth. Finally, I pack my books and walk to the bus stop.

Read each paragraph idea below. Write a topic sentence for a paragraph about each subject.

1. Homework: _____

    _____

2. Camping: _____

    _____

3. Breakfast: _____

    _____

4. Neighbors: _____

    _____

5. Gardening: _____

    _____

Proofreading Practice:
Topic Sentences

As you read the article below, read the sentences carefully. Draw a line under the topic sentences in each paragraph.

The Titanic

The "unsinkable" British ship, the *Titanic*, hit an iceberg and sank on its maiden voyage. It was traveling from England to New York City. It was about 1,600 miles from New York City when what was believed to be the safest ship afloat sank in the early morning hours of April 15, 1912.

Why did the *Titanic* sink? Sixteen watertight compartments had been built in its hull to prevent this tragedy. If two compartments should flood, a steel door would keep water from filling the others. This system failed. When the ship struck the iceberg, a gash was created in the side of the ship. The steel hull fractured, and six of the compartments flooded. The great ship went down.

Safety features for ships improved after this disaster. New laws were passed regarding lifeboats, ship radios, and ice patrols. All this was done to be sure a tragedy like this one would never happen again.

Writing Sentences
that Keep to the Topic

Find two details that don't belong in the picture above. Write them on the lines below.

_____

_____

In a picture, the details should all fit the main idea. The same thing is true of a paragraph. When you write a paragraph, make sure that all of your detail sentences tell about the main idea of your paragraph.

Writing Sentences that Keep to the Topic

Read the following paragraphs. Underline the topic sentence in each. Then draw a line through each sentence that doesn't tell about the main idea.

What an exciting game we played last Saturday! The score was tied in the ninth inning with a runner on third. Donna came up to bat. She has red hair. Soon there were two strikes against her, and we were ready to call it quits. Then she hit the pitch well and beat out the throw. Our winning run scored.

The triangle-players went over their parts one more time. The first trumpet-player loosened up his lips with two runs up and down the scale. The kettle-drummer, testing for tone, tapped his big copper tubs quietly. Tickets to the band concert were quite expensive. The band members were getting ready to play.

Uncle Jake loves to make unusual sandwiches. One of his favorites is peanut butter, tuna, and banana on toast. Did you ever watch a monkey eat a banana? He almost always uses peanut butter on his sandwiches. He says it helps hold everything together.

Write On Your Own

Write a paragraph of your own on another sheet of paper. Choose one of the topics below or think of your own. Be sure that all of your detail sentences tell about the topic of your paragraph.

My Favorite Salad   Caring for a Pet

A Funny Dream   My Secret Hideout

Support Sentences

- The topic sentence gives the main idea of a paragraph.
- The **support sentences** give the details about the main idea.
- Each sentence must relate to the main idea.

Read the paragraph below. Underline the topic sentence. Cross out the sentence that is not a support sentence. On the line, write a support sentence to go in its place.

> Giving a surprise birthday party can be exciting, but tricky. The honored person must not hear a word about the party! On the day of the party everyone should arrive early. A snack may ruin your appetite.

_____

Read each topic sentence. Write three support sentences to go with each.

Giving a dog a bath can be a real challenge!

1. _____

2. _____

3. _____

I can still remember how embarrassed I was that day!

1. _____

2. _____

3. _____

Computers are now a part of everyday life.

1. _____

2. _____

3. _____

Topic Sentences

Read each topic listed below. Write a topic sentence for each topic.
Example: Topic: Seasons
Topic Sentence: There are four seasons in every year.
or: Of all the seasons, my favorite is summer.

1. Topic: Winter
Topic Sentence: _____

2. Topic: Skateboards
Topic Sentence: _____

3. Topic: America
Topic Sentence: _____

4. Topic: Horses
Topic Sentence: _____

5. Topic: Books
Topic Sentence: _____

Choose two of your best topic sentences from above. Write each as the beginning sentence for the two paragraphs below. Write at least four support sentences to go with each topic sentence to make two complete paragraphs.

_____
_____
_____
_____
_____
_____
_____
_____
_____

Paragraph Form

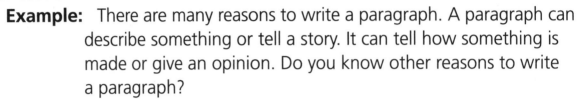

- A **paragraph** is a group of sentences about one main idea.
  When writing a paragraph:
    1. **Indent** the first line.
    2. **Capitalize** the first word of each sentence.
    3. **Punctuate** each sentence.
        Example: There are many reasons to write a paragraph. A paragraph can describe something or tell a story. It can tell how something is made or give an opinion. Do you know other reasons to write a paragraph?

Read the paragraph below. It contains errors. Rewrite the paragraph correctly on the lines by following the three basic rules:

1.**Indent**.   2.**Capitalize**.   3.**Punctuate**.

> the number of teeth you have depends on your age a baby has no teeth at all gradually, milk teeth, or baby teeth, begin to grow later, these teeth fall out and permanent teeth appear by the age of twenty-five, you should have thirty-two permanent teeth.

_____

_____

_____

_____

_____

_____

Proofreading Paragraphs

It is important to be able to edit, or proofread, things that you write to correct any errors.

Read each paragraph. Proofread for these errors:
- indentation
- punctuation
- capitalization
- spelling
- sentences which do not belong (mark out)

Rewrite each paragraph correctly on the lines.

---

my brother will graduate from high school this week everyone is so excited for him Many of our relatives are coming from out of town for his graduation Our town has a university. mom and Dad have planed a big surprise party

---

_____

_____

_____

_____

---

riding in a hot-air balloon is an incredible experience first, everyone climbs into the basket the pilot then starts the fuel which produces hot air and gradually the hot air inflates the ballone which begins to rise The road leads to an open field to lower the balloon, the pilot gradually releases air

---

_____

_____

_____

_____

Paragraph Plan

When writing a paragraph it will help to follow a basic plan.
Look at the example below.

Paragraph Plan

Step 1: Choose a topic.

Step 2: Brainstorm for ideas.

Step 3: Write a topic sentence.

Step 4: Use ideas from Step 2 to write support sentences.

Step 5: Write the topic and support sentences together in paragraph form.

Example

Step 1: Helping with household chores

Step 2: Cleaning room
Taking out trash
Washing dishes
Feeding pets

Step 3: Most kids help their families with household chores.

Step 4: Some kids take out the trash every day. Many kids like to feed their pets or help with the dishes. Almost every kid has to keep a neat room.

Step 5: Most kids help their families with household chores. Some kids take out the trash every day. Many kids like to feed their pets or help with the dishes. Almost every kid has to keep a neat room.

Write On Your Own

On another piece of paper, use the paragraph plan to write a paragraph. Choose a topic from the group of ideas below.

My Favorite Food, Being a Good Friend, or Staying Healthy

Step 1: Topic
Step 2: Ideas
Step 3: Topic Sentence
Step 4: Support Sentences
Step 5: Write Paragraph

Writing Paragraphs

Number each phrase below:

1 if the phrase tells who Mr. Mahooney is.
2 if it tells what he did.
3 if it tells why he did it.

_____ funny, old man

_____ because he had no home

_____ patched, colorful coat

_____ walked through the park

_____ talked and laughed with children

_____ big smile

_____ sat on bench

_____ bright blue eyes

_____ because he had no children

_____ fed birds

_____ because he enjoyed the park

_____ because he enjoyed talking to others

Use the above ideas to write three paragraphs about Mr. Mahooney. Write one paragraph for each number. Continue writing on another page if necessary.

_____

_____

_____

_____

_____

_____

_____

_____

_____

_____

_____

_____

Proofreading Practice:
Paragraphs

As you read the report below, you will notice that the report has not been divided into paragraphs. Read the sentences carefully. Use the proofreader's mark (¶) beside each sentence that starts a new paragraph. (Hint: There sould be four paragraphs in this report.)

Australia

Australia is unique because it is the only country that is also a continent. It is often called the "Land Down Under" because it lies solely in the Southern Hemisphere. The first settlements in Australia by the British government were made in 1788, using British prisoners. Great Britain had lost the War of Independence in the U.S. and had to find a new place to send the convicts from its overcrowded jails. Therefore, the prisoners were sent to this island country to serve their sentences. The warm, dry climate and an abundance of good grazing land soon attracted other settlers. Australia has a number of unusual animals. Along with about 700 species of birds and about 140 species of snakes, Australia has the world's only black swans, the koala, the kangaroo, the platypus, and the wombat. Australia is divided into six states. Its capital is Canberra. Some of Australia's larger cities are Sydney, Brisbane, Adelaide, and Melbourne.

Proofreading Practice:
Paragraphs

As you read the report below, you will notice that the report has not been divided into paragraphs. Read the sentences carefully. Use the proofreader's mark (¶) beside each sentence that starts a new paragraph. (Hint: There sould be four paragraphs in this report.)

Olympic Games

The Olympic Games attract the best athletes from almost every country in the world to compete in a series of events. The modern Olympics were organized to promote the ideal of a "sound mind in a sound body" and to encourage world peace and friendship among nations. The five interlocking rings of the Olympic symbol represent the continents of Asia, Africa, Australia, Europe, and North and South America. At least one of the five colors of the rings is included in the flag of every nation. The Olympic Games are separated into the Summer Games and the Winter Games. A major city always hosts the Summer Games, while the Winter Games are always held at a winter resort. The Summer and Winter Games take place on a four-year cycle, two years apart. For example, the Winter Games are scheduled for 2002, and every four years after that. The Summer Games are scheduled for the year 2004, and every four years thereafter.

Comparison Paragraph

Often it is important to compare two or more things. In a **comparison paragraph** you will write about how the things are alike and different. You can compare people, places, things or ideas.

Before writing it may be helpful to brainstorm.

Example: Comparing cars and buses

Likenesses	**Differences**
Both are vehicles.	Buses are much larger.
Both carry people.	Fewer people ride in cars at
Both travel on streets.	one time.
Both have engines, motors,	People pay fares to ride buses.
bodies, wheels, etc.	Cars are owned by people.
Both run on fuel.	

Use these ideas to write two paragraphs to compare cars and buses. The topic sentences are already written for you. Write one paragraph about likenesses and one about differences.

Cars and buses may have more in common than you might think.

_____

_____

_____

Although cars and buses are alike in many ways, there are still many differences

between them. _____

_____

_____

Compare: **TV** and **movies**

Brainstorm:

Likenesses	**Differences**
_____	_____
_____	_____
_____	_____

Definition Paragraph

- Sometimes you may write a paragraph to define something. A **definition paragraph** tells exactly what something is, without sounding like a dictionary.

    Example: An *opera* is a play in which the actors sing their lines. An opera can tell a story about any subject. The music is written to help express the feelings of the story. Together, the words and music make opera a wonderful experience!

- It is easier to describe a thing than a feeling or attitude. These descriptions are much more personal.

    Example: *Confidence* is a feeling of being sure about something or someone. I feel confident in myself when I do well at school. I feel confident about my family and friends because I know that I count on them for their help and friendship.

Use these guidelines to write a paragraph to define each word.
    Ask yourself: 1. What does it look like? or…How does it feel?
                        2. What does it do?
                        3. How does it affect me? or…How is it used?

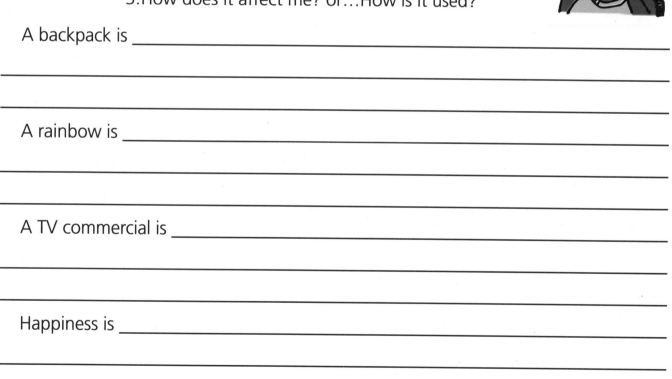

A backpack is _____

_____

_____

A rainbow is _____

_____

_____

A TV commercial is _____

_____

_____

Happiness is _____

_____

_____

Descriptive Paragraph

- A **descriptive paragraph** tells about something that is observed or experienced.
  A good description makes a word picture for the reader.

  Example: The banana split was an ice cream lover's dream come true.

 A large, blue, oval dish was lined with long slices of bananas. On the bananas were three huge scoops of ice cream: chocolate fudge, vanilla, and strawberry. Drizzled over the vanilla scoop was loads of hot fudge sauce. Butterscotch sauce was dripping down the other two scoops. And lastly, chopped nuts were sprinkled over the sauce, with a puff of whipped cream and a cherry to top it off!

Read each topic below.

| My Favorite Outfit | My Best Friend | Riding a Skateboard |
| My Pet | Riding a Roller Coaster | My Favorite Outdoor Place |

Choose two topics. Make a list of details that could describe each one.

Topic 1. _____   **Topic 2.** _____

_____   _____

_____   _____

_____   _____

_____   _____

Write a topic sentence for one of the topics above. Use your details from each list to write support sentences to make a good descriptive paragraph.

_____

topic sentence

_____

_____

_____

_____

Explanatory Paragraph

- An **explanatory paragraph** tells how to do something.
  Example: cook spaghetti, build treehouse, wash car, study for test

Use the plan below to write an explanatory paragraph. Before writing your paragraph, organize your ideas below.

Topic: _____

I. What materials are needed? _____

_____

_____

II. What is the step-by-step plan? (in order) _____

_____

_____

III. What are the final results? _____

_____

_____

1. Choose a topic.
2. Write a topic sentence that tells what will be explained.
3. Write a sentence that tells what materials are needed.
4. Write sentences that give steps in the correct order
   (Remember to use "time" and "sequence" words. Example: today, tomorrow, first, last).
5. Write sentences to give special details.
6. Conclude with sentence that tells the final results.

How to _____

_____

_____

_____

Expository Paragraph

- An **expository paragraph** gives detailed information, either facts or opinions or both.

> **Example:** My favorite sport is swimming. It not only is fun and refreshing on a hotday, but it is also a great way to exercise. I go swimming almost every day in the summer.

Write an expository paragraph on each subject to tell…

All About Me

My favorite pastime is _____

_____

_____

I think my family is super because _____

_____

_____

Summer is important to me because _____

_____

_____

When I grow up, I want to be a _____

_____

_____

If I could be anywhere in the world, _____

_____

_____

My favorite way to spend a Saturday afternoon _____

_____

_____

Persuasive Paragraph

- You probably have strong opinions about many subjects. A **persuasive paragraph** is a way to express strong opinions and to try to make others feel the same way. You may have strong feelings about current events, clothes, homework, chores, TV shows, pollution, or many other topics.

Think of a topic that you feel strongly about in a positive way, and a topic you feel strongly about in a negative way.

Follow these steps to write a persuasive paragraph about each topic.
1. Choose a topic.
2. Write a topic sentence that states your strong opinion and why you feel this way.
3. Write several supportive sentences that give your reasons. Try to include several facts as well as feelings.
4. End with a sentence that summarizes your strong opinion.

I. Topic_____ (Positive opinion)

_____

_____

_____

_____

_____

_____

II. Topic _____ (Negative opinion)

_____

_____

_____

_____

_____

_____

_____

Writing About Pictures in Sequence

Do you ever read comic books? Comic book picture stories are drawn in a special order. That special order is called **sequence**. Sequence tells what comes first, next, and last.

The pictures below are drawn in sequence. They tell part of a picture story. Think about what the pictures show. Then draw a picture in the last space to complete the story.

First   Next   Last

Now write three sentences that describe the pictures of the girl. Be sure to write your sentences in sequence.

First _____

_____

_____

Next _____

_____

_____

Last _____

_____

Writing About Pictures in Sequence

The pictures below are not in sequence. Put the pictures in sequence so that they show a story. Write first, next, or last under each correct picture.

_____ _____ _____

Now write three sentences that describe the picture story above.

First _____

Next _____

Last _____

Write On Your Own

On another sheet of paper, draw a picture story of your own. Use three or more pictures for your story. Then, under each picture, write a sentence that describes it. Be sure your pictures and sentences are in sequence. You may use one of the ideas below, or you may think up your own idea.

    Flying a Plane

    Making a Pizza

    Scoring a Point in a Game

Writing with Sequence Words

Look at the pictures.

Before

After

Certain words always tell sequence. They are called **sequence words**. *Before* and *after* are sequence words. Some other sequence words are *first*, *then*, *next*, *last*, and *finally*.

Read the next paragraph. Then underline the sequence words in it.

> Mel looked at the painting, first with his head tilted to the left, then with it tilted to the right. Next he tried squinting at the painting. Finally he decided the painting was okay if you liked smashed fruit.

Writing with Sequence Words

The following paragraph uses sequence words. But the sequence of events is backwards. Rewrite the paragraph on the lines below by starting with the first event and ending with the last event. Change the sequence words so that they tell the correct order.

> The elegant Lester LeMouche strolled down the avenue to his favorite restaurant. Before that, he splashed aftershave on his jaw and threaded a rosebud through the buttonhole in his jacket. And before that, he got dressed. Earlier he showered and shaved. At first, he peered at his pocket watch and saw that it was dinner time.

_____

_____

_____

_____

_____

_____

_____

_____

Write On Your Own

On another piece of paper, write a paragraph about your future. Tell about your plans. Write about what you might be doing two years from now, five years from now, and ten years from now. Use sequence words and circle each sequence word that you use.

Writing About Activities in Sequence

Are you one of those people who find it hard to get organized in the morning? Or do you follow a certain sequence?

Here are some things most people do every morning. On the lines below, write them in a sequence that makes sense.

eat breakfast   put on a coat
turn off the alarm   get out of bed
get dressed   brush your teeth

First, _____

Second, _____

Third, _____

Fourth, _____

Fifth, _____

Last, _____

Writing About Activities in Sequence

Imagine that while you're walking on the beach you see a bottle washed ashore. It has a message inside. What's the message? Write it on the line.

_____

Now think about where the bottle came from. Did it come from a boat, a desert island, a faraway land — or from your friend who likes to play jokes?

Write a paragraph about how the bottle got to the beach. Tell who wrote the message and when. Tell some details about the bottle's journey. Be sure your sentences are in sequence.

_____

_____

_____

_____

_____

_____

_____

_____

_____

Write On Your Own

What is your favorite game? How do you play it? On another sheet of paper, write a paragraph about the game using sequence words to describe how it is played.

Combining Sentences

- Combining sentence parts when you revise your writing can make a sentence smooth and can cut out extra words as well.
    Babe is a video I really like. *Pinocchio* is good, too. *Matilda* is one of my favorites.
    Babe, *Pinocchio*, and *Matilda* are three of my favorite videos *or* I really like *Babe*, *Pinocchio*, and *Matilda*.

Practice

You do not need all the words in the following sentences to say what you want to say. Rewrite each group of sentences on the line to make one well-combined sentence.

1. I loved *James and the Giant Peach* by Roald Dahl. I also loved *Matilda* by Dahl.

   _____

2. *Oink* was illustrated by Arthur Geisert. Geisert illustrated *Haystack*, too.

   _____

3. *Jumanji* is a really weird story. *Bad Day at Riverbend* is strange, too.

   _____

4. *The Book of Hot Lists for Kids* gave me some great ideas for things to do. *The Kids' Summer Handbook* taught me some things, too.

   _____

   _____

5. Books make my weekends fun. CDs also give me some fun things to do.

   _____

Combining Sentences

- If you are saying two things about the same person or place, you can often combine these parts into one sentence. Do this by using more than one verb in a sentence.

    Our class **planted** a garden. We **weeded** the garden, too.

    Our class **planted and weeded** the garden.

    We **found** a video about crops the Inca planted. We **watched** the video.

    We **found and watched** a video about crops the Inca planted.

Practice

Combine each pair of sentences into one sentence that has two verbs. Write the new sentence on the line.

1. Nancy Ward thought about her Cherokee people. She worried about them.

_____

2. Nancy talked to the leaders. She begged them to listen to her.

_____

3. She led her people. She showed them a way to survive.

_____

4. Nancy also talked to the white people. She showed them how they could have peace.

_____

Combining Sentences

* You can improve a piece of writing by using one exact word in place of a whole sentence.

  The parrot has beautiful feathers. They are very **colorful**.

  The parrot has beautiful, **colorful** feathers.

  Bats eat mosquitoes and other insects. Bats are **useful** creatures.

  Useful bats eat mosquitoes and other insects or Bats are **useful** because they eat mosquitoes and other insects.

Practice

Combine the sentences in each pair. Write a new sentence by adding a single word from one sentence to the other.

1. My aunt doesn't like this winter weather. It's cold almost every day.

   _____

2. She often wears unusual winter clothes. She wears colorful winter clothes.

   _____

3. On really cold days, she wears a fluffy jacket. The jacket is purple.

   _____

4. She also wears a cap with a pom-pom on top. The cap is made of wool.

   _____

5. She says she likes her winter clothes. They are warm.

   _____

Combining Sentences

- You can combine sentences by using a phrase in place of a wordy sentence. A **phrase** is a group of related words that does not have a subject or verb.

> My friend taught me step dancing. She grew up in Ireland.
>
> My friend **from Ireland** taught me step dancing.
>
> That man enjoys watching the dancers. He uses a cane.
>
> That man **with the cane** enjoys watching the dancers.

Practice

Change one sentence into a phrase and place it in the other sentence. Write the new sentence on the line.

1. We watched our neighbor walk by. She led a beautiful dog.

   _____

2. Our neighbor seems friendly. Her house is that brick one.

   _____

3. The Newfoundland puppy is hers, too! It has a floppy ear.

   _____

4. She and the dog are going on a hike. She wants to reach Crater Lake.

   _____

5. She walks the dog every day. The dog wears a leash.

   _____

Combining Sentences

- You can combine two sentences with these words: **and**, **but**, and **or**. The two parts of the combined sentence are separated by a comma.

  Many people drive to work, **but** people in cities often use public transportation.

  Cars pollute the air, **and** gas for a car may be expensive.

  You can choose to fly long distances, **or** you can drive for several days.

Practice

Combine these pairs of sentences using **and**, **but**, or **or**. Write the new sentence on the line. Be sure to add a comma.

1. Trains have crossed the United States since the 1860s. They have moved millions of people.

   _____

   _____

2. Today many people still love to ride the train. Many others think it is too slow.

   _____

   _____

3. Many families think driving is the easiest for them. It can be tiring.

   _____

   _____

4. Many people with babies choose to drive. They can fly faster.

   _____

   _____

Combining Sentences

Practice

Practice combing sentences below.

1. The quarter rolled under the sofa.
   The dime rolled under the sofa.

   _____

2. The fourth graders are in the school play.
   The fifth graders are in the school play.

   _____

3. The kids went to the library.
   The kids checked out books.

   _____

4. The sandwiches are in our picnic basket.
   The chips are in our picnic basket.

   _____

5. Katy folded her camp clothes.
   Katy packed them in her luggage.

   _____

6. Mom came to my school's Open House.
   Dad came to my school's Open House.

   _____

7. All the guests ate refreshments.
   All the guests had a great time.

   _____

8. Our teacher gave us a math assignment.
   Our teacher told us to work quietly.

   _____

Combining Sentences

When sentences are short and choppy, they can be combined into one good sentence. Combine each group of sentences below into one sentence. The first one is done for you.

1. Three children played ball. They jumped rope. They were happy.

   <u>Three happy children played ball and jumped rope.</u>

2. These marbles are bright. They are shiny. They are mine.

   _____

3. The movie was long. It was funny. I liked it.

   _____

4. Those are fishing boats. They are old. They sail out on the ocean.

   _____

5. The day is windy. The day is cloudy. It is rainy.

   _____

6. The purse was black. It was stolen. It was not found.

   _____

7. Lee's dog has a red collar. He is lost. He is black.

   _____

8. The window is dirty. It is broken. It is stuck.

   _____

Combining Sentences

Two sentences can be written as one sentence by using connecting words. Read the two sentences. Choose one of the words to the left to combine the two sentences into one sentence.

1. We can eat now. We can eat after the game.

   while
   or
   because
   _____
   _____

2. We stood on the cabin's deck. The sun rose over the deck.

   as
   or
   but
   _____
   _____

3. Sarah wanted to watch TV. She had lots of homework to finish.

   because
   when
   but
   _____
   _____

4. The concert did not begin on time. The conductor was late arriving.

   until
   because
   while
   _____
   _____

5. The spectators cheered and applauded. The acrobats completed their performances.

   when
   if
   but
   _____
   _____

6. The baseball teams waited in their dugouts. The rain ended and the field was uncovered.

   or
   until
   after
   _____
   _____

Friendly Letter

A **friendly letter** is a casual letter between family or friends. A friendly letter can express your own personality. It can be written for a special reason or just for fun.

Write a friendly letter to a "friend" in another city. Invite the friend to visit you some time during the summer. Follow these guidelines:

A. Heading: Write your address and date. (your street name and number on the first line; your city, state abbreviation and zip code on the second line)

B. Greeting: (**Example:** Dear (Fill in name of person to whom you are writing.))

C. Body: Write three paragraphs.
   First: pleasant greeting and invitation
   Second: details about visit
   Third: summarize excitement about visit

D. Closing (**Example:** Your friend)

E. Signature (your name)

A _____

B _____

C _____

D _____

E _____

Business Letter

Read the letter below. Notice the spacing and form of the letter. Notice also the names of the parts of the letter.

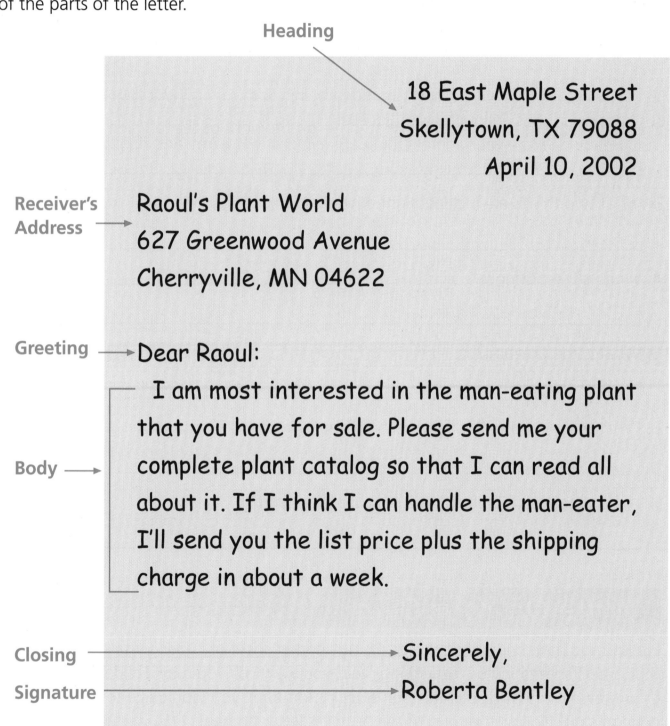

Heading

18 East Maple Street
Skellytown, TX 79088
April 10, 2002

Receiver's Address

Raoul's Plant World
627 Greenwood Avenue
Cherryville, MN 04622

Greeting

Dear Raoul:

Body

I am most interested in the man-eating plant that you have for sale. Please send me your complete plant catalog so that I can read all about it. If I think I can handle the man-eater, I'll send you the list price plus the shipping charge in about a week.

Closing

Sincerely,

Signature

Roberta Bentley

Business Letter

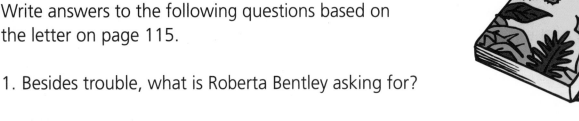

Write answers to the following questions based on
the letter on page 115.

1. Besides trouble, what is Roberta Bentley asking for?

_____

2. Where is the receiver's address written — on the right or the left side of the page?

_____

3. What two things are included in the heading?

_____

4. What is the closing?

_____

5. What is the greeting?

_____

6. What punctuation mark follows the greeting?

_____

7. In what part of the letter is the purpose expressed?

_____

Write On Your Own

Pretend you have one million dollars. Using another sheet of paper, write a business letter
that orders something or many things that you want. Or you may decide to give the
money away. In that case write your letter to someone you would like to receive your
generous gift. Follow the form of the business letter on page 115.

Proofreading Practice:
Addressing Envelopes

Now that you have learned how to write a letter, you need to learn how to address an envelope. In the upper right corner of the envelope, write your name. Below your name, write your street address followed on the next line by your city, state, and Zip code. In the center of the envelope, write the name of the person to whom you are writing. On the line below the person's name, write that person's street address followed by the person's city, state, and Zip code. Remember to capitalize the names of people and places. Also notice the comma placed between the city and state.

Dr. B. J. Morris
Granville Hospital
1814 Riverside Street
Columbus, OH 43206

Ford Motor Company
201 Henry Ford Drive
Detroit, MI 62805

Look at the envelope below. Correct the capitalization and punctuation. Use the envelope above to help you.

megan cullen
275 daisy lane
boston ma 02101

mr. timothy parlette
917 south market
las vegas nv 89109

Writing an Invitation

An invitation must give all the necessary information. It must at least answer the questions **who**, **what**, **when**, and **where**.

Write an invitation using the information below.

WHO: (person you are inviting)
             (your name)
WHAT: A surprise party
WHEN: Saturday, March 12, at 2:00 p.m.
WHERE: 1112 Circle Drive

Getting Started with the Writing Process

1. **Selecting**, or choosing, a subject is the first step in the writing process. Let's say you want to write about your dog, Buster. First, write *Buster* and draw a circle around it, like this: (Buster)

   Now put six spokes on your circle.

2. Next you need to **collect** your ideas. Do this by putting a word or words at the end of each spoke that tell something about Buster. Draw a circle around each set of these new words. The more ideas you collect, the easier it will be to write your story.

3. Now you are ready to **connect**, or group, all your ideas that tell about the same thing. *Long ears* and *one black eye* describe how Buster looks. Put those ideas together. *Barks loudly* and *waits for me* tell about things Buster does. Connect those things next. Now connect the tricks that Buster knows. As other ideas come to you, add more spokes and put them in new circles. This will help you shape and organize your writing.

4. Your next step will be **drafting** your thoughts into paragraphs or a report. Start writing about the ideas you have connected. Write about only one group of ideas at a time.

5. Now you should **revise** your writing. Delete unnecessary information and correct errors in mechanics, usage, and grammar. Share your corrected copy with a parent or friend. Ask your parent or friend to suggest other improvements.

6. After you have made all the changes you feel are necessary, you are ready to write your final copy. Be sure to **proofread** it.

Tips for Your Own Writing:

- **Select** a subject.
- **Collect** your ideas.
- **Connect** all your ideas into paragraphs.
- **Draft** your ideas into paragraphs.
- **Revise**, revise, and revise again!
- **Proofread** your final copy.

Getting Ideas

The best ideas for writing come from **your** experiences, opinions, and imagination. Ask yourself what you like and care about. List those things. Next, ask yourself what things interest you and what you would like to know more about. Make a list of those things. You now have two lists of ideas!

Look at your two lists and circle the idea that is most interesting to you. Put that idea in a circle on a new sheet of paper. Think about that idea. Draw spokes around the circle and put ideas or details describing your idea at the ends of the spokes and circle them. Select the ideas or details you want to use. It is not necessary to use all of them. Now connect, or group, those ideas that tell about the same thing.

You are ready for your first draft. Write by using the details in the circles. Write quickly and do not revise yet. Experiment if you wish, but remember to be yourself. When you are finished, revise and then proofread. You are the expert!

Tips for Your Own Writing:

- Make a list of things that are important to you, and circle your favorite topic from the list.
- Write all your thoughts about that circled topic.
- Select which ideas you want to use.
- Connect the ideas.

Writing a Paragraph

The **beginning** of your paragraph introduces your main idea. You can use one fact, statement, topic, or belief to introduce your main idea or topic. If you stick to your topic, it helps control your writing. A good paragraph is about only one idea and is supported by examples, reasons, or descriptions.

The **middle**, or the body, of the paragraph is where you expand on the main idea by using explanations, descriptions, or details to support it. You arrange those specific details or explanations in some type of logical or effective order. If you are describing the inside of your house, you might describe one room at a time. That would be using spatial order, or space. Sometimes you use chronological order, which means you explain what happened in the same order that it happened. You can also expand your main idea by selecting the details according to their order of importance.

The **closing** of your paragraph is the ending. It comes after the details and explanations in the body. The closing sentence usually reminds the reader what the topic is about. It also makes your paragraph complete.

Tips for Your Own Writing:

- Put only one idea in a paragraph.
- Write specific details about your topic.
- Arrange the details in a logical or effective order.
- Indent when you start a new paragraph.

Staying on Topic

Each paragraph deals with only one idea. Watch out for sentences that wander from the main idea. Get rid of them. They confuse readers. Read the paragraph below. It has a good introduction. Why did the writer include the sentences shown in red?

> The day that I broke my arm started out like most days. I struggled out of bed and ate breakfast. Then I looked at the kitchen clock. It was the new clock we gave Mom for Mother's Day. I had only three minutes to get to the bus stop! I grabbed my book bag and flew out the door. I wish I had seen our dog standing outside the door. We got our dog at the animal shelter. I tripped over her and landed on the cement steps. The rest of the story is too painful to tell!

Each sentence in red has something to do with the sentence just before it. One sentence tells more about the clock. The other tells more about the dog. However, these two sentences have nothing to do with the topic of the paragraph. They do not tell how the writer broke his arm. Take these two sentences out of the paragraph. What kind of an ending sentence does the paragraph have? Does it make the writing seem complete? Although it doesn't tell what happened next, it does tell you why the writer decided not to go on with the story.

Tips for Your Own Writing:

- Read each sentence in your writing and ask, "Does this sentence belong in this paragraph? Does it tell more about the main idea of the paragraph?"
- You may find that the sentences you take out belong in another paragraph.

Proofreading Checklist

To get mistakes out of your writing, proofread! You can use the proofreading marks on page 6 of this book.

Look for one or two mistakes at a time. First, read your writing out loud, word for word. That makes it easier to spot any missing or extra words. Next, check to see if any words need to have capital letters. Remember, each new sentence should begin with a capital, and all names begin with a capital. Maybe you used a capital letter and you shouldn't have. Now see if each sentence has an end mark. Are all words spelled correctly? Look at the words that give you trouble. Ask a friend to proof your paper for you. Your friend may see something you missed. Here is how one writer marked the mistakes in her writing:

> Do you remember your first day in forth grade? I do. my family had just moved to northville. I didn't have any friends yet. When I got to School, a boy was waiting for me at the front door. He knew my my name! I was so surprised! He said his name was jeremy. He would show me my homeroom. I was alredy happier!

Tips for Your Own Writing:

Can your writing pass this test?
- Did I spell all words correctly?
- Do any sentences have missing or extra words?
- Did I start all sentences and proper nouns with capital letters?
- Do all sentences end with a period, question mark, or exclamation point?
- Did I indent each paragraph?
- Can I tell what each paragraph is about?

Narrative-Descriptive Story

A narrative is a story, either true or imagined. Its purpose is to tell about an event or series of events. Narration usually includes a great deal of description. The plan of a narrative is developed through a **beginning**, a **middle**, and an **end**. The **beginning** of a story usually introduces the people or characters, and the place and time period (setting). The **middle** of the story usually shows the characters doing something (generally facing a problem) when a conflict (the main problem) arises. The **end** of the story shows how the characters deal with or solve the conflict. Remember, every story does not have a happy ending.

Description helps the reader picture a person, place, or thing. It deals with the appearance or nature of a person, place, or thing. Select the details of your description to paint a picture with words so that the reader can not only see, but also smell, touch, hear, or taste what you are describing. All details should be concrete and clear, showing color, sound, and motion. Use description throughout the story to paint clear pictures that make your readers feel as if they are there inside your story.

Tips for Your Own Writing:

- Think of a problem your characters can solve.
- Know your characters. Imagine what they like and dislike. What personality traits make them different and interesting?
- Plan a beginning to your story where you introduce the characters and setting.
- Plan a middle by deciding on the main problem the characters will face and how they will deal with it.
- Plan an end by deciding how the conflict or problem will be dealt with or resolved.

Expository-Planning a Report

Expository writing is used when you write a report. It is used to tell what a thing is, how it works, its history, and how its parts relate to each other. Follow the first two steps of the writing process to make planning a report easier.

1. **Selecting**—It is best to choose a subject that is interesting to you. Ask yourself what you would really like to know about the topic that you have chosen. Make a list of questions you would like to answer. Research your topic. For instance, if the general topic is fish, you might decide to narrow your topic to a certain kind of fish, like barracuda.

2. **Collecting**—
   a. **Gather** interesting facts and details about your subject. Encyclopedias, books, magazines, on-line computer services, videotapes, and slides are all good sources of information.

   b. **Take notes** about important facts and details. To help you with this, you might want to go back to the list of questions that you wrote in step 1. Write each question at the top of a different note card. When you find a fact or detail that helps answer the question, write it in your own words on the note card. Be sure to write the source of your information.

Sample note card:

What do barracuda look like?
• long body
• sharp set of fangs and jutting lower jaw
• great barracuda may grow to more than 10 ft in length
Evans, T.S. *All About Barracuda*. Columbus: McGraw-Hill, 1996

   c. **Organize** your information by choosing one of your note cards to be the main focus of your report. Arrange the rest of your note cards with your focus in mind. Use the information on the main note card to write the first sentence of your report.

Tips for Your Own Writing:

- Make sure there is enough information about your topic.
- Write each question that you want answered at the top of a note card.
- Write facts and details about each question in your own words.

Expository-Writing a Report

If you followed the steps for proper planning, the writing of your report should not be difficult. Now follow the next two steps of the writing process.

Connecting your facts and details involves the writing of your first draft. Arrange your note cards in an order that links the answers to one question with the answers of another. Play around with your note cards until you come up with an order that pleases you. Then, write your draft, writing not only what is on your note cards but what you remember as well. You do not need to copy the questions at the top of each card. As you write, you may think of another way to look at your subject.

Now look at your opening paragraph. It should interest the reader. It should also contain the main idea of your report. If it doesn't, rewrite it.

After you have written your report, write a closing paragraph. Make sure you summarize the main points to leave your readers with a good idea of what your whole report is about. After you have written the first draft, read it aloud to make sure it flows smoothly. Check each paragraph to see if the ideas are arranged in the best possible order. Remember to use your own words, not those of the books you read, and present your facts as clearly as possible.

Before asking another person to read the report and suggest changes, check your spelling, capitalization, and punctuation. Revise and edit the report as many times as you feel it needs it. Now it is time for the final stage of the writing process: **proofreading**.

Ask a parent or friend to proofread your report to check for spelling, usage, capitalization, and punctuation. Copy your report, making any changes that are needed.

Tips for Your Own Writing:

- Write a first draft, connecting information from your note cards and your memory.
- Write an opening paragraph and a closing paragraph.
- Read your report and revise and correct wherever necessary.
- Have another person suggest changes to your report.
- Correct your report by taking a last look at it and writing your final copy.

Writing a Persuasive Composition

Persuasive writing tries to convince the reader to believe what the writer believes or to do what the writer wants the reader to do. To begin your writing, complete this statement, "I want to convince you that. . . ." You may finish the statement by writing, "I want to convince you that we should visit Gettysburg on our vacation." Consider who will be your reader. How can you make that reader agree with you? You need reasons that would be convincing for that reader. Reasons may be either facts or opinions. Each fact or opinion goes into a separate sentence. A fact can be proven; an opinion cannot be proven. Words like *should*, *dislike*, *delightful*, and *believe* indicate an opinion is being expressed.

Fact: Gettysburg is an important historical place.

Opinion: I believe that seeing a place where history happened makes it easier to learn about our past.

Where do you find facts? You find them in dictionaries, encyclopedias, and almanacs. You can find facts and opinions in newspapers, magazines, textbooks, the Internet, and interviews. Make sure you check your evidence to see if it supports your position. Name the persons you refer to who agree with your position. Write all the information on note cards.

It is time to look at your facts and opinions. Are your reasons convincing? If your facts are accurate and they are supported by the opinions of experts and reliable sources, it is more likely your readers will agree with you.

Conclude your paper by stating your persuasive argument again as strongly as you can. Revise and proofread your paper as often as you need to. Have a parent or friend proofread it also. Then write your final copy.

Tips for Your Own Writing:

- Is your position clearly presented?
- Have you given your reader appropriate reasons for agreeing with you?
- Do all of your reasons support your position?
- Do you conclude with a clear summary of your position and your reasons for it?

Postal State and Possession Abbreviations

Use these abbreviations on envelopes to be read by postal workers. In other writing, spell out the names of the states.

States

Alabama ....AL
Alaska ....AK
Arizona ....AZ
Arkansas ....AR
California ....CA
Colorado..CO
Connecticut ....CT
Delaware..DE
Florida..FL
Georgia..GA
Hawaii ....HI
Idaho ....ID
Illinois IL
Indiana...IN
Iowa ....IA
Kansas ....KS
Kentucky..KY
Louisiana..LA
Maine ....ME
Maryland ....MD
Massachusetts....................................MA
Michigan..MI
Minnesota..MN
Mississippi..MS
Missouri ....MO
Montana...MT
Nebraska..NE
Nevada ....NV
New Hampshire..................................NH

New Jersey...NJ
New Mexico.......................................NM
New York ....NY
North Carolina ....NC
North Dakota ....ND
Ohio ....OH
Oklahoma..OK
Oregon ....OR
Pennsylvania ....PA
Rhode Island ....RI
South Carolina ....SC
South Dakota ....SD
Tennessee ....TN
Texas..TX
Utah...UT
Vermont...VT
Virginia ....VA
Washington ....WA
West Virginia......................................WV
Wisconsin ....WI
Wyoming ....WY

District of Columbia ....DC

U.S. Possessions

American Samoa.................................AS
Guam ....GU
Puerto Rico ....PR
Virgin Islands.....................................VI

Capitalization
People and Pets

- The word **I** is always capitalized.
  I think it's important to take good care of pets.

- The names of people always begin with a capital letter.
  A pet's name should also be capitalized.
  My cousin **J**ason adopted a dog from the animal shelter.
  The dog is only about ten inches long, but **J**ason named her **T**erminator.

Practice

Read the sentences below. Circle each word that should begin with a capital letter.

> I saw a puppy that would make a great pet. His ears stand up like wolves'
> ears do, so (i) think we should name him (wolf) My older sister (colleen) is learning
> to be a veterinarian, and she will help me learn about taking care of a large dog.
> Since (wolf) is a malamute, we visited a man who raises these great dogs. A dog
> named (iditarod) followed us around. The man, whose name is Jake, explained
> that (iditarod) is named for a dogsled race in Alaska. Malamutes are working dogs.
> We would have to give (wolf) a lot of exercise, even in very cold weather, and
> keep him brushed, because malamutes have thick fur. When grown, they can
> weigh about 85 pounds. (jake) said that we would have to buy a lot of dog food.
> We're thinking about that.

7

Capitalization
People's Titles

- Titles, such as **Mr.**, **Mrs.**, **Miss**, **Ms.**, and **Dr.**, are often
  included with a person's name. When used as part
  of someone's name, titles and their abbreviations
  are always capitalized.
  Dr. Mary Faber talked to our class about first aid.
  Mr. Sherman is the new gym teacher.

- A word that just shows relationship should not be
  capitalized. Words such as **my**, **your**, **his**, **her**, **its**, **our**,
  or **their** come before a word that just shows relationship.
  My **g**randfather seems to do everything really well.

  However, if a word that shows relationship is used in
  place of a name, or with a name, it should be capitalized.
  "**G**randfather," I said, "you certainly are a better fisherman than I am."
  "Well," he answered, "**A**unt **M**innow catches more fish than any of us."

Practice

Read the paragraph below. Circle the four words that should be capitalized.

> Celia Sandoz grew up in western Nebraska. Her grandfather was Jules Sandoz,
> a very early settler in the region. Celia's father was also named Jules. Celia had
> always heard stories about (grandfather) Jules's family, who had a very difficult
> life. Celia's aunt, Mari Sandoz, became a famous writer. Once, (aunt) Mari wrote
> a book called *Winter Thunder*. It was about Celia's adventure during a rare
> blizzard in Nebraska. The famous (ms.) Sandoz also wrote a biography of her
> father. Travelers today can see the home of (mr.) Jules Sandoz.

8

Capitalization
Titles of Written Works

- The important words in the titles of books, stories,
  poems, songs, movies, and plays should always begin
  with capital letters. The important words are all words
  except conjunctions (*and*, *but*, *or*), articles (*a*, *an*, *the*),
  and prepositions (*on*, *in*, *at*, *of*, *by*).
  Have you read **R**ing of **B**right **W**ater? It's a book
      about otters.
  The old song "There's a **H**ole in the **B**ucket" is fun to sing.
  We always watch **W**here in the **W**orld Is **C**armen **S**andiego?

- Capitalize an article, conjunction, or preposition if it is the first or last word in a title.
  I saw the play **T**he Wizard of Oz.
  "**A**t the Seaside" is a poem by Robert Louis Stevenson.
  Josh read **A**nd to Think That I Saw It on Mulberry Street to his brother.

Practice

Read each sentence. Circle the capitalization mistake in each title.

1. Artist Marilyn Hafner drew funny pictures for the poem "(an) Only Child"
   by Mary Ann Hoberman.
2. Tales of (A) Fourth Grade Nothing is my favorite book by Judy Blume.
3. Did you ever read the book Chicken Soup (With) Rice by Maurice Sendak?
4. One of Lettie's favorite books is The (gold) Cadillac by Mildred Taylor.
5. Stephen's choir sang "Swing (low,) Sweet Chariot" at the winter concert.
6. A good book about stars is The Sky Is Full (Of) Stars by Franklyn Branley.
7. Casey gave the book Why (In) the World? to her dad for his birthday.
8. Our class went to see the play The Man Who Loved to (laugh.)

9

Capitalization
Places

- Some place-names refer to any one of a
  group of places, such as streets, cities,
  countries, continents, islands, oceans,
  and deserts. These names do not need
  to be capitalized.
  There are many **m**ountains and **o**ceans in the world.

- Other place-names refer to a specific place. These names should be capitalized.
  The **R**ocky **M**ountains are in **N**orth **A**merica.
  The **H**awaiian **I**slands have a warm climate.

Practice

Read the following paragraph. Circle the seven place-names that should be capitalized.
Then write them correctly on the lines below. You may need to use a United States map
to help Teresa solve "The Best State" mystery.

> On a dusty attic wall, Teresa discovered a faded map. "The Best State" it said
> on the map. "What's the best state?" Teresa wondered. She read the small print
> carefully. There were many names on the map. She saw (helena) and (billings) She
> found (flathead lake) (clark fork river) and some other rivers and lakes. She found
> (bighorn mountain) and then another mountain. To the right of "The Best State" were
> the words (north dakota) and at the top, the word (canada) After some investigation,
> Teresa figured out "The Best State" was _____ Montana _____

1. _Helena_
2. _Billings_
3. _Flathead Lake_
4. _Clark Fork River_
5. _Bighorn Mountain_
6. _North Dakota_
7. _Canada_

10

Capitalization
Dates, Holidays, Groups

- The names of specific days, months, and holidays begin with a capital letter.
  I believe that **M**ay will always be my favorite month.
  I love the way our city celebrates **M**emorial **D**ay!
  It's best when a holiday comes on a **M**onday.

- The names of specific organizations and events should also be capitalized.
  The **G**irl **S**couts and **B**oy **S**couts march in the parade every year.
  That weekend our town holds the exciting **L**incolnville **M**usic **F**estival.

Practice

Read the newspaper report below. Circle the words that should be capitalized.

Atlanta, Georgia, welcomed ten thousand athletes from all over the world on (july) 19, 1996. World-class athletes competed in the (summer olympic games). The people of Atlanta worked with the (international olympic committee) to plan a special schedule of events. It was the 100th anniversary of the modern (olympic games).

11

Proofreading Practice:
Capitalization

As you read the stories below, you will notice that some of the words have not been capitalized. Read the sentences carefully. Use the proofreader's mark (≡) to show which letters should be capitalized.

Walt Disney

Walter elias disney was born in 1901 in chicago, where he later studied art. In 1923, he moved to los angeles, california, hoping to become a film director or producer. When he could not find a job, he decided to produce cartoons. Disney's first success was in 1928 when a mickey mouse cartoon was released. He produced many more cartoon series with the addition of characters, such as donald duck, pluto, and goofy. He released many full-length films, such as pinocchio and fantasia. In 1955, disney opened his first theme park, disneyland, in anaheim, california. A second theme park, walt disney world, opened near orlando, florida in 1971, after disney died. Have you ever been to either of walt disney's theme parks?

12

Punctuation
Commas in Series

- Words in a series should be separated by commas.
  The five planets nearest the sun are Mercury, Venus, Earth, Mars, and Jupiter.
  Mars, Earth, and Jupiter have satellites.

Practice

Read the report below. Add commas between the words in a series.

Some modern structures are best known for their great size. The tallest dams in the United States are in Colorado, Arizona, Idaho, and Nevada. The dams in the United States that hold the most water are in Arizona, Montana, and South Dakota. The United States also has three of the world's longest bridges. They are in New York, California, and Michigan.

There were also huge structures in the ancient world. Among these were statues, gardens, sphinxes, and temples. Not all of these are still standing, but you still can see the Egyptian pyramids. All of these structures were the results of work by ancient artists, architects, engineers, and laborers.

13

Punctuation
Commas in Series

- A single sentence can contain a series of people, places, things, or ideas. Use a comma to separate the items in a series.
  Example: The chef is preparing veal, chicken, shrimp, and steak for dinner.

Write an informative sentence containing a series on each line about the topics below. Be sure to use commas to separate the words in a series. The first one is done to help you.

1. Four people in your family
   Kim, Chris, Jon, and Cody are going to see ___ _ool play._

2. Five school subjects

3. Three U.S. stat

4. Six

5. Four ___ of the year

6. Four body organs

7. Three kinds of math problems

8. Four medical professionals

9. Six planets

10. Five kinds of vegetables

Answers will vary.

14

Punctuation
Commas in Dates and Addresses

- A comma in a date separates the year from other words in the sentence.
  On July 4, 1976, the U.S. celebrated its 200th birthday.

- A comma in an address separates the name of a state from the rest of the sentence.
  The movie was filmed in Cheyenne, Wyoming.

Practice

Read the letter below. Add commas where they are necessary.

72809 East Saddle Road
Omaha, NE 68102
October 5, 2001

Dear Andrew,

You have to come next month to ride with us in the parade. Afterward, we can go to Council Bluffs, Iowa for a picnic. You also said you wanted to see Arbor Lodge. That's in Nebraska City, Nebraska, and not far away. We can also go there if you come.

Your friend,

Jenny

15

Proofreading Practice:
Commas

As you read the story below, you will notice that some commas are missing. Read the sentences carefully. Use the proofreader's mark (∧) to show where commas need to be added.

The Anderson's Family Trip

It was June 2, 2002. Andy Anderson was building model airplanes in his attic. His sister Allison, his mom, and his dad were downstairs packing for the family's cruise to Alaska. They were to leave the next morning. They carefully packed the aspirin, army blankets, aquatic flippers, antiseptics, and almanac that they would need for their trip.

The next day, when their car, an Acura, was all packed, the Andersons drove to Arizona to catch a plane to California. This is where they would board the cruise ship, U.S.S. *Alaskan*, to begin their journey. Three hours later, Allison noticed that they had forgotten to bring one last item — Andy! He was home alone, still in the attic with his airplanes! Meanwhile, Andy embarked on his own adventure— home alone, at last!

16

Proofreading Practice:
Commas

As you read the article below, you will notice that some commas are missing. Read the sentences carefully. Use the proofreader's mark (∧) to show where commas need to be added.

Soccer

Soccer is probably the world's most popular team sport. It is the national sport of several South American, Asian, and European countries. The popularity of soccer has grown in the United States in recent years.

In Great Britain, soccer is called football or association football. The word soccer comes from assoc., which is an abbreviation for association.

Each team has eleven players. These players each play a certain position. Some are defenders, and others are forwards and midfielders. The goalkeeper defends the goal and is the only player who is allowed to touch the ball with his hands. All other players may use only their head or body to kick, hit, or stop the ball.

17

Possessives
Singular and Plural

- The possessive of a singular noun is formed by adding an apostrophe and **-s**.
  Elena**'s** hat   Cass**'s** jeans

- The possessive of a plural noun that ends in **s** is formed by adding only an apostrophe.
  the teams**'** caps   the players**'** awards

- The possessive of a plural noun that does not end in s is formed by adding an apostrophe and **-s**.
  children**'s** clothing   men**'s** jackets

- The possessive of a hyphenated noun is formed by adding an apostrophe and **-s** to the last word.
  his brother-in-law**'s** jacket

Practice

Write the correct possessive form above each underlined word.

Liz thought it would be cool to visit the past. She thought her great-grandmothers ^{great-grandmother's} quilt was beautiful. She wondered how hard the women ^{women's} work was if they had to take time to make quilts. Did a farm familys ^{family's} day begin early? Were the children ^{children's} chores hard? Would she ever know her ancestors' stories?

18

Proofreading Practice:
Possessives

As you read the article below, you will notice that apostrophes have not been added to show possessives. Read the sentences carefully. Use the proofreader's mark (∨) to show where apostrophes need to be added. For extra practice use proofreader's marks to correct the errors in capitalization and punctuation that also appear.

Benjamin Franklin

Benjamin franklin was one of americas most famous citizens. He ran a print shop in philadelphia, where he published a newspaper, the pennsylvania gazette, and poor richards almanac. The almanac contained bens wise sayings, such as "a penny saved is a penny earned." He also organized public institutions, such as the first subscription library and americas first city hospital. As a scientist, he demonstrated that lightning is actually electricity. As an inventor, franklin gave us bifocal lenses for glasses, the lightning rod, and the franklin stove. As a statesman, franklin helped write the declaration of independence and served as minister to france. Ben died in 1790, at the age of 84.

19

Contractions

- A contraction is a shorter way to say and to spell two words. When you write, you use an apostrophe to show where you have left out a letter.
  The computer store **was not** open that evening.
  The computer store **wasn't** open that evening.
  You are learning to use your computer.
  You're learning to use your computer.

- In questions, the order of words may be changed when a contraction is used.
  Can you **not** understand why we need a computer?
  Can't you understand why we need a computer?
  Why **did** she **not** listen during class?
  Why **didn't** she listen during class?

Practice

Look at the underlined words in each sentence. They can be combined to form contractions. Write each contraction on the line at the end of the sentence.

1. The class had not visited Shedd Aquarium before. ____hadn't____
2. It is home to thousands of beautiful fish. ____It's____
3. Do not tap on the glass. ____don't____
4. That is very disturbing to the fish. ____That's____
5. At the Shedd, there is a giant squid hanging from the ceiling. ____there's____
6. You can not see some of the fish because they hide so well. ____can't____
7. You will want to go to the main aquarium at feeding time. ____You'll____
8. A diver will get into the tank; she will feed the fish. ____she'll____
9. They are from many different parts of the world. ____They're____

20

Proofreading Practice:
Contractions

As you read the article below, you will notice that some of the words are italicized. Read the sentences carefully. Rewrite the italicized words as contractions. For extra practice, use proofreaders marks to correct the errors in capitalization and punctuation that also appear.

The History of Basketball

basketball was invented by a man named james naismith he was a physical education teacher at a YMCA school in springfield massachusetts he was told to create an indoor team sport for the winter season naismith asked a janitor to nail two boxes to the gym's balcony opposite each other to be used as goals the janitor however *could not* find boxes, so he nailed up peach baskets instead the new sport then became known as basketball
the first official basketball game *was not* played until january of 1892 it was played with a soccer ball each team had nine players the game was slow-moving because each time a basket was made, someone had to climb a ladder to retrieve the ball over the years changes came about, such as a bottomless net basket, backboards, a larger ball, and some rule changes basketball gradually became the popular sport it is today

couldn't *wasn't*

21

Homophones
Your/You're, Its/It's

- **Your** is a pronoun that shows possession. It always comes before the name of something or someone.
  We saw **your** cousin at the show yesterday.
  Was she wearing **your** hat?

- **You're** is a contraction. It is the shortened form of the two words "you are." The apostrophe means that the letter a is missing from **are**.
  You're going to the show tomorrow, aren't you?
  I'll bet **you're** going to be early, as usual!

- **Its** is a pronoun that shows possession. It always comes before the name of something.
  Its mane was huge and made the lion look scary.

- **It's** is a contraction. It is the shortened form of the two words "it is." The apostrophe means that the letter i is missing from **is**.
  It's very clear that the lion is dangerous.

Practice

Write **your**, **you're**, **its**, or **it's** in each space in the following report.

If ___you're___ a computer user, you know that when a problem arises with ___your___ computer it is called a "bug." ___It's___ a term that was first used more than fifty years ago when a computer malfunctioned. The programmer found a dead moth in ___its___ interior. ___Its___ presence there was probably not the cause of the problem. If you have a problem with a computer, ___you're___ not going to be able to blame moths. ___It's___ probably not ___your___ fault, either.

22

Homophones
There/Their/They're, Here/Hear

- **There** may mean "in that place," or it may be used to introduce a sentence before a word such as **was**, **were**, **is**, or **are**. The word **here** is in the word **there**, which may help you remember.
  We found the treasure chest right over **there**.
  There were pieces of gold in the chest.

- **Their** means "belonging to them."
  The pirates said the chest was **their** property.

- **They're** means "they are."
  They're not going to like it if we take their treasure.

- **Here** may mean "in this place," or it may be used to introduce a sentence.
  Let's leave the treasure **here**.
  Here is the map that we used.

- **Hear** means "to listen." The word **ear** is in **hear**, which may help you remember.
  Didn't you **hear** the pirates' warning?

Practice

Read the sentences below. Write **their**, **there**, or **they're** in each space.

Many people work hard to develop <u>their</u>₁ muscles. <u>There</u>₂ are some muscles that you can control. <u>They're</u>₃ called voluntary muscles. <u>There</u>₄ are also involuntary muscles, which you cannot control.

Write **here** or **hear** in each space.

<u>Here</u>₅ is a fact you may not know. You have about 700 muscles. Would you like to <u>hear</u>₆ more information about your muscles?

23

Proofreading Practice:
Homophones

As you read the article below, you will notice that some words have been used incorrectly. Read the sentences carefully. Circle the words that are incorrect. Write the correct word above each word that you circled.

Whale or Fish?

The most observable difference between whales and fish is the tail. Fish have vertical tail fins and whales have horizontal tail fins. *There* (Their) are other differences. Fish breathe through *their* (they're) gills, while whales breathe through *their* (there) lungs. Whales can hold their breath for long periods under water. When they need air, they come to the surface and breathe through the blowhole on the top of *their* (they're) *its* head. A fish lays (it's) eggs, while a whale gives birth to live young. Whales are warm-blooded. Fish are cold-blooded and a fish's body is covered with scales. A whale has smooth rubbery skin. Whales are also much larger than most fish.

24

Articles
A, an, and the

An article is a kind of adjective. There are only three articles: a, an, and the.

- **A** and **an** are indefinite articles because they refer to any one of a group of nouns.
  A small plane and **an** unexpected storm made Beryl Markham's flight dangerous.

- Use the word **a** before words that begin with a consonant sound. Use **an** before words that begin with a vowel sound.
  Markham had been **a** pilot in Africa for many years.
  A compass is a useful tool.
  She had flown in **an** open cockpit plane through all kinds of weather.
  She waited **an** hour before taking off.

- **The** is a definite article because it identifies a specific noun.
  Beryl Markham was **the** first person to fly solo across the Atlantic Ocean from east to west.

Practice

Write the correct article **a**, **an**, or **the** in each sentence.

Elephants from Africa are <u>the</u>₁ ones with large, fanlike ears. Elephants also live on <u>the</u>₂ continent of Asia. <u>An</u>₃ elephant has <u>an</u>₄ almost hairless body. It also has <u>a</u>₅ long, flexible trunk. Elephants are <u>the</u>₆ largest mammals that live on land. <u>The</u>₇ only larger mammals, whales, live in the ocean.

25

Proofreading Practice:
Articles

As you read the report below, you will notice that some of the articles have been used incorrectly. Read the sentences carefully. Circle the articles that are used incorrectly. Then write the correct article above each word you circled.

Volcanoes

the
What do Mount Pinatubo in (a) Philippines, Mount St. Helens in Washington, Kilauea in Hawaii, and Mount Vesuvius in Italy have in common? They are all volcanoes.

Volcanoes are created when magma, which is hot melted rock from inside the *a* *a* earth, is forced upward. It rises through cracks and collects in (an) magma chamber. *a* *a* Pressure builds until the magma forms (an) channel through (an) broken or weakened *an* part of the rock. Then it blasts out (a) opening called a central vent. Lava, hot gases, and ash spew out onto the land. *the* Lava is (an) magma that flows onto (a) earth's surface. Lava build-ups can form mountains, such as Mount Shasta in California and Mauna Loa in Hawaii.

26

Sentence Recognition

A sentence is a group of words which expresses a complete thought.

Look at the group of words below. Write **S** in the blank if the words express a complete thought and **NS** if the words do not express a complete thought.

- S 1. A greenhouse is a building.
- NS 2. Mostly glass windows and a glass roof.
- NS 3. The lighting in the greenhouse.
- S 4. The building is not green.
- S 5. It is colorless.
- NS 6. Many green things in the greenhouse.
- S 7. The glass protects the plants.
- S 8. In winter a greenhouse is heated.
- S 9. Much care is needed for the plants.
- S 10. Plants are cared for each day.
- S 11. Bugs are sometimes a problem.
- NS 12. Greenhouse with many different areas.
- S 13. Spray all plants twice a year.
- S 14. Plants can be grown during any season.
- NS 15. Many families in the north.
- NS 16. Some vegetables by the door.
- S 17. You can harvest vegetables in a greenhouse.
- S 18. When spring comes plants may be removed.
- S 19. Watch them grow.

27

Ending Sentences

A sentence needs a good ending. Write an ending to complete each sentence.
Example: Our teacher is absent today <u>because he is sick.</u>

1. The kids arrived too late for the movie so
   _____

2. Some of the campers began to build a campfire while
   _____

3. The orthodontist wants her to wear braces until
   _____

4. The class arrived early for the mus~~
   _____

5. Our tow~~   ~~though
   _____

6. The s~~   ~~g suddenly when
   _____

Answers will vary.

7. We can meet either at the ticket stand at the game or
   _____

8. Tomorrow our summer vacation is over so
   _____

9. I will bring my music tapes to your house and
   _____

10. The hiker's leader checked his compass while
    _____

28

Beginning Sentences

A sentence needs a good beginning. Write a beginning to complete each sentence.
Example: <u>The kids ate pizza</u> and cake at the party.

1. _____ but first
   she must finish her homework.

2. _____ so the
   mailman left the package by the front door.

3. _____ and put
   them away in the closet.

4. _____ or we can
   go to a movie

5. _____ while her
   broth~~   ~~n the walk.

Answers will vary.

6. _____ if we
   can't find the key to the house.

7. _____ although
   the weatherman predicted a sunny day.

8. _____ until it
   was time for the plane to take off.

9. _____ because
   I was home in bed sick with the flu.

10. _____ so she
    ordered a pepperoni pizza instead.

29

Sentence Identification

- A **statement** tells something or gives information.
  Example: The ball game was delayed because of rain.

- A **question** asks something.
  Example: Would you like to learn to windsurf this summer?

- A **command** tells someone to do something.
  Example: Tell everyone to be ready at five o'clock.

- An **exclamation** shows strong feeling or excitement.
  Example: Look out behind you!

Read each sentence. Write a word from above on each line to name the kind of sentence.

1. statement — Our school is giving a concert next Monday.
2. question — What time does it begin?
3. command — Take these tickets to your teacher.
4. exclamation — We hope to sell five hundred tickets!
5. question — How many kids are in the orchestra?
6. statement — My brother plays the clarinet.
7. command — Don't be late for practice.
8. command — Give the cello to Kim.
9. statement — I want to take violin lessons next year.
10. statement — The band will practice Thursday afternoon.
11. question — Will you help us set up the stage?
12. question — Where are the music stands?
13. command — Don't step on that flute.
14. command — Raise the curtain.
15. statement — The conductor is ready to begin.

30

Sentence Punctuation

- A **statement** ends with a period. (.)
- A **question** ends with a question mark. (?)
- A **command** ends with a period. (.)
- An **exclamation** ends with an exclamation point. (!)

Read each sentence. Write the correct punctuation in each ☐.

1. Every Saturday morning we help a neighbor [.]
2. Would you like to help us this Saturday [?]
3. Be at my house at 8:00 [.]
4. You can help me gather the supplies we will need [.]
5. I won't be late [!]
6. Today we are raking Mrs. Ray's yard [.]
7. That elm tree is huge [!]
8. Take these lawn bags to Bob and Eric [.]
9. Tell Jan and Pat to mow the back yard [.]
10. Will you help them rake the back yard [?]
11. Don't mow too close to the flowers [.]
12. Look at that big gazebo [!]
13. Mrs. Ray has left lemonade there for us [.]
14. I will mow the front yard [.]
15. Will you sweep the front walks [?]
16. Go ask Mrs. Ray to come see her clean yard [.]
17. She thinks the yard looks super [.]
18. What will we do next Saturday [?]

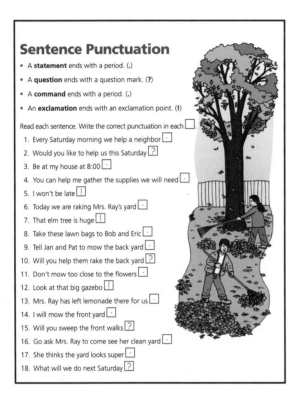

31

Writing Sentences

Put a ✔ by each correctly written sentence. Put an **X** by the sentences which contain errors. Rerite the sentences correctly on the lines below.

1. [X] the evening sky was filled with stars
2. [✓] My committee has agreed to meet next Wednesday.
3. [X] the tiny mouse ran under the table
4. [X] all of the runners were exhausted at the finish line
5. [✓] There were thirty kids at Brian's birthday party.
6. [X] what is your favorite musical instrument
7. [X] we will be late unless we hurry
8. [X] do you like to read biographies of famous people
9. [✓] The spectators cheered the winning team.

1. The evening sky was filled with stars.
2. (Sentence written correctly.)
3. The tiny mouse ran under the table.
4. All of the runners were exhausted at the finish line.
5. (Sentence written correctly.)
6. What is your favorite musical instrument?
7. We will be late unless we hurry!
8. Do you like to read biographies of famous people?
9. (Sentence written correctly.)

32

Writing Sentences

Look at the scene below. Write two of each kind of sentence to go with the picture.

Statement
1. _____
2. _____
Question
1. _____
2. _____
Command
1. _____
2. _____
Excla
1. _____
2. _____

Sentences will vary.

33

Describing with Your Senses

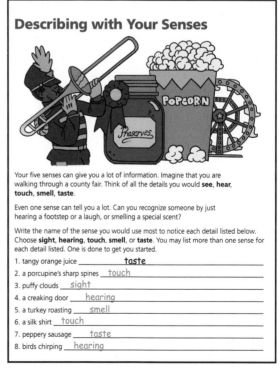

Your five senses can give you a lot of information. Imagine that you are walking through a county fair. Think of all the details you would **see**, **hear**, **touch**, **smell**, **taste**.

Even one sense can tell you a lot. Can you recognize someone by just hearing a footstep or a laugh, or smelling a special scent?

Write the name of the sense you would use most to notice each detail listed below. Choose **sight**, **hearing**, **touch**, **smell**, or **taste**. You may list more than one sense for each detail listed. One is done to get you started.

1. tangy orange juice ___**taste**___
2. a porcupine's sharp spines ___touch___
3. puffy clouds ___sight___
4. a creaking door ___hearing___
5. a turkey roasting ___smell___
6. a silk shirt ___touch___
7. peppery sausage ___taste___
8. birds chirping ___hearing___

34

Describing with Your Senses

Imagine you are walking inside a deep cave. Your way is lighted by a single candle. Suddenly a drop of water from the roof of the cave puts out the candle. Write five sentences about how you get out of the cave. You'll have mainly your sense of touch to guide you so be sure to include details about touch.

Sentences will vary.

Write On Your Own

Imagine you are a raccoon sniffing around a park. You come across a picnic lunch which is spread out on a blanket on the grass. No one is around. On a separate piece of paper, write five sentences with details describing all the delicious things you smell and taste.

35

Nouns

- A **noun** is a word that tells who or what did the action or was acted upon by the verb in the sentence.
  The scientists search for the **bones** of **dinosaurs**.
  They use soft **brushes** to remove the **dirt**.

- Nouns can be singular or plural.
  They found a small **bone** next to those large **bones**.

- Some nouns, called proper nouns, name a specific person, place, or thing: *Paul Sereno* and *South America*. They are always capitalized. Nouns like fossils are common nouns. They are capitalized only at the beginning of sentences.
  Paul Sereno found many important fossils in **South America**.

- Proper nouns may be made up of a group of words.
  The **Museum of Natural History** houses dinosaur bones.

Practice

Find the twenty-nine nouns in the following report. Circle each noun you find. Some nouns are made up of more than one word, like *prairie dogs*.

The (Badlands National Park) is in (South Dakota). Its (rocks) (woods) and (hills) were shaped by (wind) (rain) (frost) and (streams). The (hills) are surrounded by (grass). Many (animals) live there. (Visitors) can see (deer) (bison) (antelope) (coyotes) and (prairie dogs). (People) live in the (Badlands) too. (Ranchers) work on this dry (land). (Rangers) patrol the (park). (Men) and (women) run (stores) (hotels) and (restaurants).

36

Writing More Exact Nouns

What makes sentences interesting and fun to read? One thing is the words a writer chooses. For example, the sentence below would be more interesting if it had more exact nouns.

The <u>animal</u> played a <u>game</u> with the <u>person</u>.

Sentences will vary.

Rewrite the sentence in two ways on the lines above. Use more exact nouns for each noun that is underlined. Choose from the nouns below or think up your own exact nouns.

Animal: kangaroo, tiger, canary, dolphin
Game: tag, checkers, musical chairs, baseball
Person: rock singer, explorer, princess, dentist

Here are some other nouns. Think of at least three more exact nouns for each. Write them on the lines. *Suggested answers given.*

1. Bird:	cardinal	finch	chicadee
2. Color:	red	blue	orange
3. Flower:	rose	daisy	carnation
4. Sport:	soccer	football	cycling
5. Vegetable:	carrot	turnip	spinach
6. Building:	library	house	apartment
7. Furniture:	couch	bookcase	bed

37

Writing More Exact Nouns

Choose the more exact noun to complete each sentence below. Circle the noun you choose.

1. I went into the (building, (barn)).
2. There were several ((horses), animals) inside.
3. I brought a (vegetable, (carrot)) for each one.

Rewrite the sentences below. Change the nouns that are underlined to more exact nouns.

The <u>person</u> went into the <u>building</u> to buy <u>vegetables</u>, <u>meat</u>, and <u>fruit</u>. At the checkout counter, the <u>worker</u> gave her only a <u>coin</u> in change. "<u>Things</u> are so expensive," she thought, as an <u>expression</u> crossed her face.

Nouns will vary.

38

Pronouns

Writers use pronouns to avoid using nouns over and over again.

- A **pronoun** can refer to a person, a place, or a thing. The words *she*, *her*, and *it* are pronouns.
  Franny raced toward **Franny's** goal. Franny knew **the goal** was a mile away.
  Franny raced toward **her** goal. **She** knew **it** was a mile away.

- The form of a pronoun changes depending upon how it is used in the sentence. The pronouns *I*, *myself*, *my*, and *me* all refer to the same person.
  I wanted to hike there by **myself**, but **my** parents wouldn't let **me**.

- Sometimes pronouns make writing confusing. A reader cannot tell if *his* in the first sentence refers to Carl or Jacob. The second sentence makes it clear.
  Carl told Jacob to bring **his** coat.
  Carl said, "Bring **my** coat, Jacob."

Practice

Underline any words that should be changed to pronouns to make the writing smoother and clearer. Write the pronouns above the nouns.

Terri was flying in a hot-air balloon faster than the leader had promised. The
wind above the town felt cold. Terri felt uncomfortable and scared. This kind
of flying wasn't what the leader had said flying would be, Terri thought. Then
another thought came into Terri's mind. The leader hadn't said how Terri could
stop flying. Terri remembered a plastic tool in a jeans pocket. Would it help?

39

Adjectives

- An **adjective** is a word that describes a noun or pronoun. An adjective is a word that can fit in both these blanks:
  The _____ tree is very _____ .

- In the following sentence, the words **smooth**, **dark**, **big**, and **green** are adjectives.
  The artist had **smooth**, **dark** skin and **big**, **green** eyes.

- Adjectives usually come before the words they describe. Sometimes two or more adjectives describe the same word. Adjectives may tell **how many**, **what kind**, or **which one**.

- Adjectives sometimes follow a verb.
  The bicycle was **rusty**.

- Adjectives should be specific. They should help give the reader a clear picture of whatever is being described.

Practice

Circle the twenty-three adjectives in the following paragraph.

The unexpected visitors left their enormous, wooden boats and waded through
the rough, warm water to the shore. The visitors were tall and had pale skin.
Their dark, long hair was tied back with red, blue, and brown cord. The men's
bright clothing covered their bodies. Their wet faces showed that they were tired.
The first man to touch shore wore a red cape and a blue hat. He carried a long,
black stick, which he pointed at the surprised people standing on the sandy,
white shore.

40

Choosing Exact Adjectives

The sentence doesn't tell you much about Sally's sweater. Is it colorful, well-made, warm, soft? Adjectives like *nice* are not exact. Choosing exact adjectives can help make your meaning clear.

Each sentence that follows gives a choice of two adjectives. Circle the one you think makes the sentence clearer.

1. That medicine tastes (odd, bitter).
2. The (bad, vicious) dog bit its owner.
3. We saw our breath in the (icy, cold) air.
4. Returning the money was the (good, honest) thing to do.
5. I like the beach on a (nice, sunny) day.
6. The figure in the dark cape seemed (mysterious, funny).
7. The golden, jeweled crown was (pretty, magnificent).

41

Choosing Exact Adjectives

Instead of repeating the same adjectives in a paragraph, try using **synonyms**. Synonyms are words with almost the same meaning. You probably know many adjectives that are synonyms.

Each word in the first column below has a synonym in the second column. Draw a line to connect the two synonyms.

correct   tiny
awkward   peculiar
lucky   clumsy
little   fortunate
odd   right

Draw a picture of something you like (your bike, computer, a friend, etc.). Write a short description of the picture. Choose exact adjectives to describe the things in the picture.

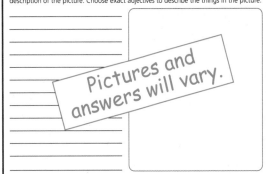

Pictures and answers will vary.

42

Expanding Sentences

Expand these sentences by adding all the given adjectives. The first one is done for you.

1. They bought the _____ stove.

   antique   black   rusty

   They bought the rusty, black, antique stove.

2. The _____ mailman just rode past.

   whistling   friendly   young

   The young, friendly, whistling mailman just rode past.

3. A _____ truck woke the baby.

   garbage   noisy   orange

   A noisy, orange, garbage truck woke the baby.

4. The Brown's _____ fence is sagging.

   wire   ugly   high

   The Brown's ugly, high, wire fence is sagging.

5. Where is my _____ shirt?

   monogrammed   blue   short-sleeved

   Where is my short-sleeved, blue, monogrammed shirt?

6. They dreamed about a _____ cake.

   sweet   chocolate   luscious

   They dreamed about a luscious, sweet, chocolate cake.

7. My _____ cap is in the cabin.

   wool   fuzzy   red

   My fuzzy, red, wool cap is in the cabin.

8. Did you find my _____ pen?

   plastic   felt-tipped   red

   Did you find my red, plastic, felt-tipped pen?

9. I would like a pair of _____ boots.

   cowboy   new   brown

   I would like a pair of new, brown, cowboy boots.

43

Overused Words

It is easy to use certain words again and again. Try giving these "tired" words a break! Read each overused word below. Write five synonyms for each. You may want to use a thesaurus.

1. wonderful _____

2. beautiful _____

3. good _____

4. okay _____

5. many _____

Answers will vary.

Read the sentences below. Choose a synonym from your list above to replace each underlined word. Rewrite the sentences using the new words.

Last Friday our class had a <u>wonderful</u> time at the Tropical Gardens. We saw <u>many</u> flowers, trees, and plants. The exotic birds were <u>beautiful</u>. We had a <u>good</u> guide. He said it was <u>okay</u> to take lots of pictures.

Answers will vary.

44

Descriptive Sentences

Turn a good sentence into a great sentence by using more descriptive words.

Example: The couple cut the cake.
The **newlywed** couple cut the **five tier** wedding cake.

Read each sentence. Add descriptive words to make each a great sentence. Write the improved sentence on each line.

1. The man climbed the mountain.

2. The group found a buried tomb.

3. The girls ...

4. The sun ... through the window.

5. Ice cream dripped down the cone.

6. The snake moved down the tree.

7. The storm rocked the boat.

Answers will vary.

45

Writing Details from Pictures

Details are small bits of information. Details tell how things look, sound, smell, feel, taste, or seem. Exact details can make a description more interesting.

Read the paragraph below. Underline all the details you find. One has been done to get you started.

It was a <u>dry, hot</u> afternoon. An <u>old, spotted</u> pony came <u>limping slowly</u> down the <u>dirt road</u>. His <u>thick hair</u> was <u>caked with dust</u>. Suddenly, the <u>tired animal</u> stopped in his tracks. He saw a <u>giant maple tree</u> close by. Under the tree was a <u>thick patch of grass</u>. It was the perfect place to eat and rest.

Now put a check mark below the picture of the animal described in the paragraph.

1. _____   2. ✓   3. _____

46

Writing Details from Pictures

List four details you find in the picture above.

1. _____
2. _____
3. _____
4. _____

Now use you~~~~~ about the picture.

1. _____
2. _____
3. _____
4. _____

Answers will vary.

Write On Your Own

On a separate sheet of paper, write a short description of a room in your home, including details. Then draw a picture of the room, showing each detail you've described.

47

Adverbs

- An **adverb** is a word that describes a verb, an adjective, or another adverb. Adverbs tell *how, when, where,* and *how much.*

    The children giggled **wildly** as the clowns ran past.
    (*Wildly* is an adverb that describes the verb *giggled.*)
    One large clown sat **very** carefully on a tiny stool.
    (*Very* is an adverb that describes the adverb *carefully.*)
    Another clown carried a **brightly** painted banner.
    (*Brightly* is an adverb that describes the adjective *painted.*)

- Many adverbs end in *-ly: wildly, sadly, quickly, slowly.* However, some common adverbs do not: *almost, not, often, too, very.* Some adverbs are spelled like their matching adjectives: *hard, first, far.*

Practice

Find the thirteen adverbs in the following paragraph. Circle each adverb you find. Remember, an adverb will tell *how, when, where,* or *how much.*

The class had studied (seriously) to learn about the (historically) important pier. They had (finally) come to visit it, but it was (too) crowded to see much. People were packed (tightly) in the restaurants. The museum was (completely) filled with visitors. The air-conditioned bookstore felt (only) (slightly) cool (inside) because of the crowds. The lines for the rides were (ridiculously) long. Why was everybody (so) happy? Why were they all (extremely) glad that they had come to this (very) exciting place?

48

Writing with Adverbs

We went there then.
We went to the museum on Saturday afternoon.

Which sentence above gives you more information? Words like **there** and **then** are **adverbs**. They tell where and when. Word groups like **to the museum** and **on Saturday afternoon** are **adverbial phrases**. They tell where and when, but they give more exact details.

Here are some other adverbial phrases:

Where	When
under the bed	after the game
aboard the ship	before next Tuesday

Replace each underlined adverb below with an adverbial phrase that gives more information. Write your new sentence on the blank line.

1. A mosquito flew <u>somewhere</u>.

   _____

2. The bus leaves <u>sometime</u>.

   _____

3. Let's go <u>there</u> t~~~

Answers will vary.

49

Writing with Adverbs

Adverbs like **excitedly** tell how. Many adverbs that tell how are formed by adding **ly** to adjectives.

   Lydia talked excitedly about the museum.
   excited + ly = excited<u>ly</u>

Some adverbs are formed by changing the **y** in an adjective to **i**, then adding **ly**.
   clumsy + ly = clumsi<u>ly</u>

Change each adjective below into an adverb that tells how.

1. alert _____alertly_____   4. quick _____quickly_____
2. cautious _____cautiously_____   5. angry _____angrily_____
3. fortunate _____fortunately_____   6. easy _____easily_____

Write a few sentences about the museum on the previous page, or a museum you like to visit. Try to use at least two how adverbs, and two when and where adverbial phrases.

_____
_____
_____
_____
_____

Sentences will vary.

Write On Your Own

Think about another place you like to visit. On a separate piece of paper, write five sentences describing this place. Try to use adverbs and adverbial phrases to make your sentences clear and interesting.

50

Expanding Sentences

You can **s-t-r-e-t-c-h** a sentence by adding more information.

Stretch these sentences by adding words to answer each question.
  Example: The plane landed. When? The plane landed at 1:30 p.m.

1. We are all going to the airport. How?
   _____

2. I am taking three pieces of luggage. Why?
   _____

3. The passengers are lined up. Why?
   _____

4. The baggage was stacked. Where?
   _____

5. She bought, her ticket. ~~How?~~

6. We will ~~_____~~

7. The tourists brought plenty of film. Why?
   _____

8. Our flight attendant is helping us. How?
   _____

9. We will fasten our safety belts. When?
   _____

10. The plane is beginning to move. Where?
    _____

11. A delicious dinner was served. When?
    _____

12. Our cautious pilot avoided the stormy clouds. How?
    _____

Answers will vary.

51

Verbs

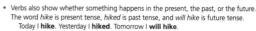

- A **verb** tells what the person, place, or thing in a sentence is doing, or it links or connects the subject to the rest of the sentence. A verb might tell about being rather than acting. The words *felt* and *hiked* are verbs.
  The boys **felt** tired as they **hiked** on the trail.

- Verbs also show whether something happens in the present, the past, or the future. The word *hike* is present tense, *hiked* is past tense, and *will hike* is future tense.
  Today I **hike**. Yesterday I **hiked**. Tomorrow I **will hike**.

- Verbs must match their subjects. In the present tense, the verb *walk* changes when its subject is a third-person singular noun, such as *girl*.
  I often **walk** on that trail.
  Girls from my school **walk** on it, too.
  I know a girl who **walks** on the trail every day.

- Some verbs express a state of being. The most common verbs that show being are *am, is, are, was, were,* and *be*.
  The cougar **was** huge, and the boys **were** terrified.

Practice

Think of a verb to complete each sentence. Remember to use the correct verb form.

Suggested answers given.

Mountain climbing ___is___ a popular sport. People ___climb___ mountains
              1   2

for many reasons. Some people ___enjoy___ the challenge of trying to reach high
                              3

and dangerous places. Others ___like___ to explore the outdoors and ___admire___
                            4   5

the beauty of nature. Whatever the reason, mountaineering ___is___ serious
                                                          6

business. Every climber ___needs___ to work with experienced teachers.
                        7

52

Subject-Verb Agreement

- In the present tense of most verbs, the endings change to match the subject. If the subject is a singular noun or the pronoun **he, she,** or **it**, the verb should end in **-s**.
  She **walks** with us.   John **walks** for exercise.
  It **walks** on its hind legs.   He **walks** with a cane.

- If the subject is a plural noun, or the pronoun **I, we, you,** or **they**, you do not add **-s** to the verb.
  They **walk** often.   I **walk** every day.
  You **walk**, too.   The workers **walk** to the fields.

- If the verb ends in **o, ch, sh, ss,** or **x**, add **-es** to the base word for singular nouns, or the pronoun **he, she,** or **it**.
  I **fish**.   Do you **fish**?   Jason **fishes** every day.

Practice

In the spaces below, write the correct forms of the verbs in parentheses.

1. A camel ___carries___ heavy burdens. (carry)

2. Camels ___live___ in Africa. (live)

3. The camel ___looks___ a little like some of its relatives in America. (look)

4. You ___know___ what a llama is, don't you? (know)

5. The furry animal ___behaves___ a little like a camel. (behave)

6. A llama, though, ___does___ not have a hump. (do)

7. A llama ___carries___ a burden, just as a camel does. (carry)

8. The animals ___carry___ many pounds at a time. (carry)

9. A herder ___watches___ the valuable animals. (watch)

53

Subject–Verb Agreement

- When the subject of a sentence is one thing or one person, except **you** or **I**, add an **-s** to the verb.
  Alan seems tired in the early morning.

- When the subject of the sentence is made up of two singular persons or things joined by **and**, use a verb that does not end in **-s**.
  Alan and his trainer seem tired when they come in.

- When the subject is made up of two words joined by **or** or **nor**, add an **-s** to the verb unless the word closest to the verb is plural.
  Neither **Alan nor his trainer seems** tired.
  Neither **Alan nor his friends waste** time.

- Take special care when a helping verb comes before its subject, as it does in many questions.
  Why **do skaters and coaches** work so hard?

Practice

Underline the words that make up the subject of each sentence. In the blank, write the correct form of the verb in parentheses.

Why ___do___ <u>readers</u> and <u>television viewers</u> get animal groups mixed up?
      1 (do, does)
Often, the <u>viewer</u> and the <u>reader</u> ___decide___ that animals are alike or
                                      2 (decide, decides)
different because of their appearance. Both the <u>cassowary</u> and the <u>emu</u>
___belong___ to the group of birds that can't fly. On the other hand, <u>koalas</u>
3 (belongs, belong)
and <u>kangaroos</u> seem different, but they both ___fit___ into the same species.
                                                4 (fit, fits)
However, the <u>bear</u> and the <u>koala</u> are different and ___raise___ their young
                                                      5 (raise, raises)
in different ways.

54

Subject–Verb Agreement

Practice

Write three sentences comparing the two vehicles in the drawing. How are they alike? How are they different?

1. _____
_____
2. _____
_____
3. _____
_____

Sentences will vary.

Practice

Write five sentences about the shepherd in the picture. Describe how he feels about his work. Use at least three of these verbs, adding correct endings: **watch**, **play**, **carry**, **walk**, **climb**.

1. _____
_____
2. _____
_____
3. _____
_____

Sentences will vary.

55

Verb Tense

• The past tense of a verb tells you that something happened in the past. The past tense of most verbs is formed by adding **-ed**.
   I love to **learn** new songs. I **learned** a funny one yesterday.

• The past tense of verbs that end in silent **e** is formed by dropping the **e** and adding **-ed**. If the verb ends with a single consonant, double the consonant and add **-ed**.
   The song was about a cowhand who had to **saddle** a horse.
   After he had **saddled** it, it refused to move.
   The cowhand tried to **plan** ways to make the horse move, but everything he **planned** failed.

• The past tense of some verbs is formed by changing the spelling of the verb.
   I like to **sing**. I **sang** the saddle song over and over.
   I **write** stories. I **wrote** a story for the school newspaper.
   I **know** that I **knew** all the words perfectly yesterday.
   I **think** I've forgotten them, but I **thought** I had them memorized.

Practice

Write the correct past tense verb above each underlined verb in the paragraph below.

> thought   was   sat
> I think television is unhealthy for kids. We sit around too much. How many
> ￼   played   Were
> of us play sports every single day? Are most teens in sports? You say that you
> skated   loved   walked   planned
> skate? You love hiking? Well, most kids walk very short distances! We all plan
>   exercised
> to exercise, right? Next week, be able to say, "I exercise every day!"

56

Verb Tense

Read the sentences below. Then write the past tense form of the verbs given.

1. Julie watches the parade. _____watched_____
2. Ted calls his horse. _____called_____
3. He walks quickly. _____walked_____
4. They play hard. _____played_____
5. Sheila dances beautifully. _____danced_____

Some verbs don't add **-d** or **-ed** to form their past tense. Instead they change spelling. For example: **fly — flew, take — took, drink — drank**. If you are not sure of how the past tense of a verb is spelled, look it up in your dictionary.

Read the sentences below. Then write the past tense form for each verb given.

1. Coreen drinks lots of fruit punch. _____drank_____
2. Robert flies his model airplane. _____flew_____
3. Barbara leaves early in the day. _____left_____
4. Jason runs fast. _____ran_____
5. We go to a basketball game. _____went_____

Practice

Use the past tense of **watch**, **run**, and **fly** in three sentences of your own.

1. _____
2. _____
3. _____

Sentences will vary.

57

Proofreading Practice:
Verb Agreement and Tense

As you read the story below, you will notice that some of the verbs are not used correctly. Read the sentences carefully. Circle the verbs that are incorrect. Write the verbs correctly making sure that the verbs you write are correct in agreement and tense.

> ### Young George Washington
>
>   moved
> George was born on February 22, 1732 in Virginia. His family move to an
>   was
> undeveloped plantation, later called Mount Vernon, when he were three years
> old. They had no nearby neighbors.
>
> George didn't receive many years of formal education. He wrote his lessons
> on sheets of paper that his mother then sewed into a notebook. His favorite
>   was   planned
> subject were math. His father had plan to send him to school in England, but
>   was
> when George were just eleven years old, his father died. George was then
> needed by his mother on the farm. At a young age, George helped manage a
> plantation worked by twenty slaves. No one
> knows
> know for sure if he really chopped down
>   was
> his father's cherry tree, but he were a quiet,
> patient, dependable, and honest young man.

58

Writing with Interesting Verbs

Look at the picture and read the sentence below.

Harry **went** up to the hurdle and **jumped** over it.

The underlined words in the sentence are verbs. Verbs express action. The verbs *went* and *jumped* tell something about what is happening in the picture. But these verbs could be more interesting. Read the next sentence that uses more interesting verbs to tell about the picture.

Harry **raced** up to the hurdle and **leaped** over it.

Read the following list of verbs. Then write two more interesting verbs for each one given. One is done to get you started. If you need help, use a dictionary.

Suggested answers given.

1. look — **peek** — **glance**
2. talked — chatted — gossiped
3. ate — gulped — dined
4. walked — sauntered — strolled
5. went — disappeared — exited
6. touched — patted — stroked

59

Writing with Interesting Verbs

All of the verbs are underlined in the sentences below. Using more interesting verbs, rewrite the sentences on the lines below. Use some of the interesting verbs that you wrote on the previous page or think up other interesting verbs.

Sam Spade <u>went</u> to the scene of the crime. He <u>looked</u> around for clues. Then he <u>walked</u> back to his office. He <u>ate</u> a sandwich quickly while he <u>moved</u> back and forth in the room. After a while, he <u>touched</u> his desk with his foot. He decided that his pet Chihuahua had <u>taken</u> his hat after all.

Verb choices will vary.

Write On Your Own

On separate sheet of paper, write five sentences about one of your hobbies. Use interesting verbs; share your writing with a friend.

60

Proofreading Practice:
Writing with Interesting Verbs

As you read the story below, you will notice that some of the verbs are italicized. Read the sentences carefully. Write a more interesting verb above each italicized verb.

Gentlemen: Start Your Engines

I'll be the first ten-year-old in history to *be* in the Indy 500. I can hear it now. Reporters will grab their microphones ___ the amazing event.

"Young Zach Rossfield ___ 500, after qualifying in the time trials ___

Zach's red-and-___ his dad and grandpa back home in Columbus ___ was no scrimping on this racer. Krazy Kid Motor Oil, Zach's sponsor, paid all expenses including Goodyear racing radials. When interviewed today, Zach *said* that he feels a little nervous about the race but plans to go home with part of the $7 million purse. He promised to keep a cool head and try his best to drive safely.

"Zach! Zach! Earth to Zach!" my friend Henry yelled, breaking me out of the best daydream I've had in ages.

"Huh?" I mumbled.

Henry *said* impatiently, "I asked if you'd like to race our go-carts after school."

Verb choices will vary.

61

Proofreading Practice:
Writing with Interesting Verbs

As you read the story below, you will notice that some of the words are italicized. Read the sentences carefully. Using the Word List, choose a better, more interesting word for each italicized word you find.

Word List

| enormous | gazing | peered | shivery | spectacular |
| rush | wailing | eagerly | clever | amazed |

Thanksgiving Day Parade

It was a *cold* [shivery] Thursday in November in New York City. Thomas *looked* [peered] out the window of his New York City condo overlooking Central Park. People were crowded on every street corner and lined every sidewalk. *Excitedly* [Eagerly] looking in the direction of the approaching floats were scores of children. Thomas heard bands playing, sirens *going* [wailing], and voices singing. What was happening here? Then Thomas followed the stares of the people *looking* [gazing] up, up, up. He was *surprised* [amazed] to see *huge* [enormous] helium balloons of every color, size, and shape. He wanted so badly to *hurry* [rush] out of his condo to see more of this *neat* [spectacular] event, but he knew he couldn't. Thomas would never be able to find his way through the crowds and make it home in time for dinner–unless he devised a very *smart* [clever] plan.

62

Adjectives that Compare

- Most adjectives can be compared by adding **-er** to compare two things, and **-est** to compare more than two.
    Hyenas are **fast** runners. Gazelles are **faster** than hyenas.
        Cheetahs are the **fastest** of all.
    A hippopotamus is a very **large** mammal, but an elephant is **larger**. The **largest** of all is the whale.

- Some adjectives are compared by placing the word **more** or **most** in front of the adjective.
    Deer are **frequent** visitors to our camp, but black bears are **more frequent** than the deer. The **most frequent** visitors are raccoons.

- To compare some adjectives, change the word completely.
    Our back porch is a **good** place to watch deer.
        The park at the edge of town is **better** than the porch.
        The **best** of all places is the beach on Summer Lake.
    The mosquitoes are **bad** this year.
        Some people say they were **worse** two years ago.
        Everyone agrees the **worst** year was 1990.

Practice

Write the correct form for each adjective shown in parentheses.

1. This path is _____ safer _____ than that one. (safe)
2. This is the _____ best _____ view in the park. (good)
3. Would you be _____ more comfortable _____ on a raft than in a canoe? (comfortable)
4. Upsetting the canoe was the _____ scariest _____ accident I ever had! (scary)
5. Ms. Jason was _____ more helpful _____ than I was. (helpful)

63

Adjectives that Compare

Practice

Using the picture below, write a sentence using a comparative form of each word in parentheses.

1. (tall) _____

    Sentences will vary.

2. (silly) _____

    Check for comparative forms:

3. (wise) _____ taller/tallest, sillier/silliest

    _____ wiser/wisest, better/best

4. (good) _____

64

Comparing Two Things

The suitcase on the left is **lighter**.
The suitcase on the right must be **fuller**.

- The sentences above are **comparisons**.
    Comparisons tell how things are alike or different.

- Comparisons often use **adjectives**. Read the underlined adjectives in the sentences above. What two letters do they end in? When two things are compared, the ending **er** is added to many adjectives.

Look at the pairs of pictures that follow. For each pair, write a sentence comparing the two things. Use the *er* form of the adjective given.

1. fat: _Sentences will vary. Check that your child has used the correct word fatter in the sentence._

Sentences will vary. Check that your child has used the
2. clean: _correct word cleaner in the sentence._

65

Comparing Two Things

- With longer adjectives, we use the word **more** to make comparisons: **more delicious, more beautiful**.

Finish each comparison below. Use words from the Word List, or think of your own adjectives. Use each adjective only once.

Word List

more expensive	faster	brighter
more playful	deeper	bigger

1. An apartment house is _____ an a cottage.
2. A kitten is _____ than a cat.
3. A car is _____ than a bicycle.
4. A lake is _____ than a puddle.
5. The sun is _____ than the moon.

Adjectives will vary.

Write On Your Own

Choose one of the pairs below to compare. Make a list of -er adjectives for each one in the pair. Then, on a separate sheet of paper, write three sentences, using the adjectives to compare the two things.

Sunday and Monday   a dog and a cat

a peach and a lemon   you and a friend

66

Comparing More Than Two Things

Brenda is the **most skillful** skier on this hill.
She reached the bottom in the **fastest** time.

Read the sentences above. They compare Brenda to some other people. The adjectives used in the sentences are the words **fastest** and **most skillful**. When we compare more than two things, we add the ending **est** or use the word **most** with the adjective.

Write a sentence that uses each adjective below. Look at the picture of the skiers to give you some ideas.

1. coldest: _____

_____

2. most awkward: _____

_____

3. most difficult: _____

_____

Sentences will vary.

67

Comparing More Than Two Things

Look at the three winners of the Centerville Dog Show. Write three or four sentences comparing the three. Use at least one adjective in each sentence. Here are some adjectives you may wish to use: **smallest**, **furriest**, **biggest**, **longest**, **most playful**.

_____
_____
_____
_____
_____
_____
_____

Sentences will vary.

Write On Your Own

Books of records often list the "most" and the "best." On a separate sheet of paper, make up your own list of at least six records. List things or people you think are the most or the best. Tell why you chose each one. Here are some ideas to get you started.

Most delicious food   Most unusual hobby

Funniest person   Most useless object

68

Writing Comparisons Correctly

- You add **est** or **most** to an adjective when you compare more than two things. But how do you know which to add? With one-syllable adjectives and many two-syllable adjectives, use *est*:
  dull, dull**est**   happy, happi**est**

- Use **most** with long adjectives. Also use **most** with adjectives that end in **ful**, **ous**, **al**, and **ish**:
  fortunate, **most** fortunate   careful, **most** careful

Read the paragraph below. In each sentence there is a choice of words in parentheses. Underline the correct form.

This part of the jungle was the (interestingest, <u>most interesting</u>). Snakes hung from the (<u>lowest</u>, most low) branches of the trees. Then we saw the (magnificentest, <u>most magnificent</u>) building we had ever seen. Surely this was the Temple of Bom Gabala, the (mysteriousest, <u>most mysterious</u>) temple in the world.

69

Writing Comparisons Correctly

Remember to use **er** or **more** to compare two items. Use **est** or **most** to compare more than two things. Each label below contains two choices. Underline the word which correctly describes the pictured item.

1. the <u>shorter</u>/shortest pencil

2. the <u>more</u>/most acrobatic dancer

3. the bigger/<u>biggest</u> lineman

Some adjectives have special forms: **good, better, best**   **bad, worse, worst**

Write the correct form of each word in parentheses.

1. Arnie is a (good) ___better___ player than I am.

2. In fact, he is the (good) ___best___ player on the team.

3. Your yard looks (bad) ___worse___ since you stopped mowing the lawn.

4. It is the (bad) ___worst___ looking yard on the block.

Write On Your Own

Write the following adjectives on a separate piece of paper: **noisy, comfortable, good, delicious, funny**. For each, write a pair of comparison sentences. In one sentence, compare two things. In the other, compare more than two things. Be sure to write the adjective forms correctly.

70

Writing Comparisons with <u>like</u> and <u>as</u>

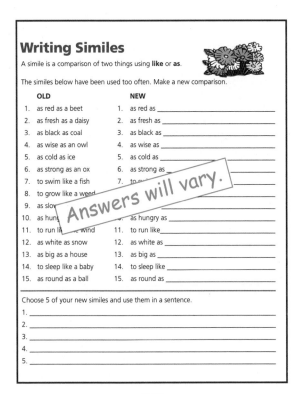

Comparing Dad to a firecracker gives a clearer and more interesting picture than just saying he's angry. A comparison that uses the word **like** or **as** is called a **simile**. Similes can help make writing clearer and more lively.

Read these similes and answer the questions.

a. My stomach feels as empty as a doughnut hole.

b. The stage was as bright as a million fireflies.

1. In simile a, the two things being compared are

      stomach   and   doughnut hole

2. In simile b, the two things being compared are

      stage   and   fireflies

71

Writing Comparisons with <u>like</u> and <u>as</u>

Now try writing some similes of your own. Complete the sentences below with the most expressive comparisons you can think of.

1. At the sound of the starting gun, Elena ran as fast as

_____

2. When I shined Pa's old boots, they _____

_____

3. The superjet stood _____ way, huge and shiny like

_____

- You can describe something with several similes, making a simile poem.

  Complete this simile poem.

    My striped scarf is as colorful as a field of tulips.

    Its wool feels soft, like _____

    It keeps me as warm as _____

    When I wear it, I look like _____

Answers will vary.

Write On Your Own

On a separate sheet of paper, write your own simile poem. Choose something you own or something you see every day. Describe the object, using three or more similes, and see how unusual and interesting this everyday object becomes. Here are some things you might describe: a pet, a bike, a tree, a building.

72

Writing Similes

A simile is a comparison of two things using **like** or **as**.

The similes below have been used too often. Make a new comparison.

OLD	NEW
1. as red as a beet	1. as red _____
2. as fresh as a daisy	2. as fresh _____
3. as black as coal	3. as black _____
4. as wise as an owl	4. as wise _____
5. as cold as ice	5. as cold _____
6. as strong as an ox	6. as strong _____
7. to swim like a fish	7. to _____
8. to grow like a weed	8. to _____
9. as slow _____	9. _____
10. as hun_____	_____ as hungry as _____
11. to run li_____ wind	11. to run like _____
12. as white as snow	12. as white as _____
13. as big as a house	13. as big as _____
14. to sleep like a baby	14. to sleep like _____
15. as round as a ball	15. as round as _____

Answers will vary.

Choose 5 of your new similes and use them in a sentence.

1. _____
2. _____
3. _____
4. _____
5. _____

73

Figures of Speech

- **Figures of speech** can make sentences more interesting. Here are four popular kinds of figures of speech:

  Personification — gives human characteristics to things.
    Example: The sun touched us with its warm fingers.
  Hyperbole — a great exaggeration.
    Example: She's the happiest person in the universe.
  Simile — compares two unlike things, using **like** or **as**.
    Example: He is hungry as a horse.
  Metaphor — only suggests a comparison of two unlike things.
    Example: The vacant field was a desert.

Read each sentence. Underline the figure of speech. Write the name of the figure of speech on each line.

Personification	1.	The <u>wind howled</u> as the storm grew closer.
Simile	2.	The little lady <u>nibbled at her lunch like a bird</u>.
Metaphor	3.	Sarah's little sister <u>was a doll</u> in her new clothes.
Hyperbole	4.	The camp leader said he would <u>never sleep again</u>.
Metaphor	5.	The banana cream <u>pie was heaven</u>.
Simile	6.	We were as <u>busy as bees</u> all day long.
Personification	7.	His <u>patience just flew out the window</u>.
Metaphor	8.	He said that his <u>life was an open book</u>.
Simile	9.	The newlyweds were <u>as happy as two lovebirds</u>.
Personification	10.	The heavy <u>fog crept slowly</u> to shore.
Simile	11.	The champion wrestler is <u>as strong as an ox</u>.
Metaphor	12.	The <u>twins were angels</u> for helping their mom.
Hyperbole	13.	I am so full that I <u>never want to eat again</u>.
Metaphor	14.	Sometimes my <u>memory is a blank tape</u>.

74

Rewriting

You already know that **proofreading** means reading over your work and correcting any errors it may have. Along with proofreading your writing, you may often have to rewrite it. Rewriting means improving your writing. You may want to use more exact nouns, verbs, or adjectives. Or you may want to put better rhythm in your writing by changing the length of your sentences. Or you just may want to make your writing clearer.

Read the following paragraph. Then read the "rewrite" of the same paragraph below. Finally write answers to the questions that follow.

> It was a good day. The sun was out. The air was nice. The trees moved in the wind. I felt very nice.

> Saturday was a delicious fall day. The sun was bright, and the air was crisp and clear. The trees rustled leaf-songs. I felt as excited as the flaming colors of red, yellow, and orange.

1. What is one more exact noun that is used in ___ *Suggested answers given.*
   Saturday

2. What more exact verb is used?
   rustled

3. What more exact adjectives are used?
   delicious, fall, bright, crisp

4. Write the first three words of the two sentences that are combined.
   The sun was, The air was

5. Do you think the rewrite is an improvement? ___ *yes*
   Why? ___ *It is more descriptive and interesting.*

75

Polishing Your Writing

Do your own rewrite of the next paragraph on the lines below. Look back at the rewrite on the previous page if you need help.

> She got up one morning. She got dressed. She had breakfast. She went outside. She played all afternoon.

Sentences will vary.

76

Writing About a Person

Use some of the words on the left to finish the character descriptions. You may also choose your own words.

honest
fearless
handsome
stubborn
graceful
depressed
gloomy
lazy
happy-go-lucky
sensible
cowardly
smiling
red-headed
tall
blonde
full mouth
turned-up nose
button nose
gray eyes
long-legged
wide shoulders
erect posture
curly hair
messy hair
tiny mouth

a four-year-old boy:
Brad is very active and eager to play. His body is very wiry.

a ten-year-old:
Na___ ___rkling blue eyes. ___ nose and ___ mouth. Her actions

Descriptions will vary.

a teenager:
This teenager is thoughtful, capable and nice to know. He

77

Finding the Main Idea

Look at the picture.

Underline the sentence below that tells what the whole picture is all about.

1. The piano player is holding her ears.

2. No one likes the man's singing.

3. There are tomatoes on the stage.

The sentence that tells what the whole picture is all about is called the **main idea**. The other sentences describe **details** in the picture. One detail of the picture is the woman holding her ears. Write another detail of the picture.

Suggested answer given.

A man throws a tomato.

Paragraphs also have main ideas and details. A paragraph is a group of detail sentences that tell about one main idea.

78

Finding the Main Idea

Read the paragraph below. Pay attention to the detail sentences.

> Marie pushed her carrots to one side of her plate. She flattened the top of her mashed potatoes and placed one carrot there. Then she cut her meat into small pieces. She put them in a circle around the mound of potatoes. "Aren't you going to eat, Marie?" her mother asked.

Now underline the sentence below that tells the main idea.
1. Marie pushed her carrots aside.
2. Marie's mother asked her a question.
3. Marie played with her food instead of eating it.

Read the next paragraph. Write two details from it. Then write its main idea.

> What a day Mr. Montez had! First the car wouldn't start. Then he found two angry customers waiting for him at the store. About noon, he got a headache that lasted all afternoon. That night, his favorite TV show was replaced by a s *Suggested answers given.*

Detail: ___The car wouldn't start.___
Detail: ___Mr. Montez got a headache that lasted all afternoon.___
Main Idea: ___Mr. Montez had a bad day.___

79

Writing a Topic Sentence

Sometimes the main idea of a paragraph is stated in one sentence in the paragraph. This sentence is called the **topic sentence**. Topic sentence is another name for the main idea.

Read the paragraph below. Think about the main idea.

> She was the prettiest horse I ever saw. Her hide shone like a polished copper kettle. Her tail streamed in the breeze when she trotted, and she tossed her head proudly.

1. Draw a line under the topic sentence. *Suggested answers given.*
2. Write two details.
   ___The horse's hide shown like a polished copper kettle; her tail streamed in the breeze when she trotted.___

The topic sentence often comes at the beginning of a paragraph. But sometimes it comes at the end or even in the middle.

Read the paragraph and the one on the next page. Underline the topic sentence in each.

> Julio started down the stairs. He was careful not to walk on loose steps that might groan under his weight. His hand gripped the rail, but not too tightly. What if it creaked? Holding his breath, he tiptoed from step to step. Finally he stood in the dark at the bottom. Julio got to the basement without making a sound.

80

Writing a Topic Sentence

> My sister doesn't like the rain. But I think rainy days can be fun. We play card games for hours, and I usually win. We dress up in old hats and capes and pretend we're old-fashioned ladies. Most of all, I like to sit on the window seat and read while rain splatters on the windowpane outside.

The topic sentence in the next paragraph is missing. Add up the detail sentences to find the main idea. Then write a good topic sentence.

> The burning sun rose higher over the city. People leaned out of windows and fanned themselves. Children sat limply on curbs. Ice cream and cold drink sellers were the only people working. *Suggested answer given.*
> ___It was an unbearably hot summer day.___

Write On Your Own

On another sheet of paper, write your own paragraph. Choose one of the topic sentences below or think of your own. Try putting your topic sentence first. Then rewrite your paragraph, moving your topic sentence to another place in the paragraph.

> I love to walk in the park in the spring.
> Photos help me to remember good times.
> My old sneakers have been good friends.

81

Topic Sentences

- A paragraph is a group of sentences that tells about one main idea. One of the sentences states the main idea. That sentence is called the **topic sentence**. The topic sentence is usually the first sentence in the paragraph.
  Example: (The topic sentence is underlined.)
      Three planets in our solar system have rings around them. The planets with rings are Saturn, Uranus and Jupiter. The rings are actually thin belts of rocks that orbit the planets. Saturn is the most famous ringed planet.

Underline the topic sentence in the paragraph below.

> Every weekday morning I follow a basic routine to get ready for school. I get up about 7 a.m., wash my face, and get dressed. Then, I eat breakfast and brush my teeth. Finally, I pack my books and walk to the bus stop.

Read each paragraph idea below. Write a topic sentence for a paragraph about each subject.

1. Homework: _____
2. Camping: _____
3. Breakfast: _____ *Answers will vary.*
4. Neighbors: _____
5. Gardening: _____

82

Proofreading Practice:
Topic Sentences

As you read the article below, read the sentences carefully. Draw a line under the topic sentences in each paragraph.

The Titanic

The "unsinkable" British ship, the *Titanic*, hit an iceberg and sank on its maiden voyage. It was traveling from England to New York City. It was about 1,600 miles from New York City when what was believed to be the safest ship afloat sank in the early morning hours of April 15, 1912.

Why did the *Titanic* sink? Sixteen watertight compartments had been built in its hull to prevent this tragedy. If two compartments should flood, a steel door would keep water from filling the others. This system failed. When the ship struck the iceberg, a gash was created in the side of the ship. The steel hull fractured, and six of the compartments flooded. The great ship went down.

Safety features for ships improved after this disaster. New laws were passed regarding lifeboats, ship radios, and ice patrols. All this was done to be sure a tragedy like this one would never happen again.

83

Writing Sentences that Keep to the Topic

Find two details that don't belong in the picture above. Write them on the lines below.

traffic light

traffic officer

In a picture, the details should all fit the main idea. The same thing is true of a paragraph. When you write a paragraph, make sure that all of your detail sentences tell about the main idea of your paragraph.

84

Writing Sentences that Keep to the Topic

Read the following paragraphs. Underline the topic sentence in each. Then draw a line through each sentence that doesn't tell about the main idea.

What an exciting game we played last Saturday! The score was tied in the ninth inning with a runner on third. Donna came up to bat. She has red hair. Soon there were two strikes against her, and we were ready to call it quits. Then she hit the pitch well and beat out the throw. Our winning run scored.

The triangle-players went over their parts one more time. The first trumpet-player loosened up his lips with two runs up and down the scale. The kettle-drummer, testing for tone, tapped his big copper tubs quietly. Tickets to the band concert were quite expensive. The band members were getting ready to play.

Uncle Jake loves to make unusual sandwiches. One of his favorites is peanut butter, tuna, and banana on toast. Did you ever watch a monkey eat a banana? He almost always uses peanut butter on his sandwiches. He says it helps hold everything together.

Write On Your Own

Write a paragraph of your own on another sheet of paper. Choose one of the topics below or think of your own. Be sure that all of your detail sentences tell about the topic of your paragraph.

My Favorite Salad	Caring for a Pet
A Funny Dream	My Secret Hideout

85

Support Sentences

- The topic sentence gives the main idea of a paragraph.
- The **support sentences** give the details about the main idea.
- Each sentence must relate to the main idea.

Read the paragraph below. Underline the topic sentence. Cross out the sentence that is not a support sentence. On the line, write a support sentence to go in its place.

Giving a surprise birthday party can be exciting, but tricky. The honored person must not hear a word about the party! On the day of the party everyone should arrive early. A snack may ruin your appetite.

Sentences will vary.

Read each topic sentence. Write three support sentences to go with each.

Giving a dog a bath can be a real challenge!

1. _____
2. _____
3. _____

I can still remember how embarrassed I was

1. _____
2. _____
3. _____

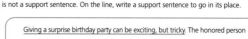

Comput___ ___ a part of everyday life.

1. _____
2. _____
3. _____

86

Topic Sentences

Read each topic listed below. Write a topic sentence for each topic.
Example: Topic: Seasons
Topic Sentence: There are four seasons in every year.
or: Of all the seasons, my favorite is summer.

1. Topic: Winter
   Topic Sentence: _____
2. Topic: Skateboards
   Topic Sentence: _____
3. Topic: America
   Topic Sentence: _____
4. Topic: Horses
   Topic Sentence: _____
5. Topic: Books
   Topic Sentence: _____

Choose two of your best ~~topic~~ ... ~~en~~ as the beginning
sentence for th~~e~~ ... four support sentences to go with
each topic se~~n~~ ... ete paragraphs.

Answers will vary.

87

Paragraph Form

- A **paragraph** is a group of sentences about one main idea.
  When writing a paragraph:
  1. **Indent** the first line.
  2. **Capitalize** the first word of each sentence.
  3. **Punctuate** each sentence.
     Example: There are many reasons to write a paragraph. A paragraph can describe something or tell a story. It can tell how something is made or give an opinion. Do you know other reasons to write a paragraph?

Read the paragraph below. It contains errors. Rewrite the paragraph correctly on the lines by following the three basic rules:

1.**Indent.**   2.**Capitalize.**   3.**Punctuate.**

> the number of teeth you have depends on your age a baby has no teeth at all gradually, milk teeth, or baby teeth, begin to grow later, these teeth fall out and permanent teeth appear by the age of twenty-five, you should have thirty-two permanent teeth.

The number of teeth you have depends on your age. A baby has no teeth at all. Gradually, milk teeth, or baby teeth, begin to grow. Later, these teeth fall out and permanent teeth appear. By the age of twenty-five, you should have thirty-two permanent teeth.

88

Proofreading Paragraphs

It is important to be able to edit, or proofread, things that you write to correct any errors.

Read each paragraph. Proofread for these errors:
- indentation
- punctuation
- capitalization
- spelling
- sentences which do not belong (mark out)

Rewrite each paragraph correctly on the lines.

> my brother will graduate from high school this week everyone is so excited for him Many of our relatives are coming from out of town for his graduation. ~~Our town has a university.~~ mom and Dad have ~~planed~~ *planned* a big surprise party

My brother will graduate from high school this week. Everyone is so excited for him. Many of our relatives are coming from out of town for his graduation. Mom and Dad have planned a big surprise party.

> riding in a hot-air balloon is an incredible experience first, everyone climbs into the basket the pilot then starts the fuel which produces hot air and gradually the hot air inflates the ~~ballone~~ *balloon* which begins to rise ~~The road leads to an open field~~ to lower the balloon, the pilot gradually releases air

Riding in a hot-air balloon is an incredible experience. First, everyone climbs into the basket. The pilot then starts the fuel which produces hot air, and gradually the hot air inflates the balloon which begins to rise. To lower the balloon, the pilot gradually releases air.

89

Paragraph Plan

When writing a paragraph it will help to follow a basic plan. Look at the example below.

Paragraph Plan	Example
Step 1: Choose a topic.	**Step 1:** Helping with household chores
Step 2: Brainstorm for ideas.	**Step 2:** Cleaning room Taking out trash Washing dishes Feeding pets
Step 3: Write a topic sentence.	**Step 3:** Most kids help their families with household chores.
Step 4: Use ideas from Step 2 to write support sentences.	**Step 4:** Some kids take out the trash every day. Many kids like to feed their pets or help with the dishes. Almost every kid has to keep a neat room.
Step 5: Write the topic and support sentences together in paragraph form.	**Step 5:** Most kids help their families with household chores. Some kids take out the trash every day. Many kids like to feed their pets or help with the dishes. Almost every kid has to keep a neat room.

Write On Your Own

On another piece of paper, use the paragraph plan to write a paragraph. Choose a topic from the group of ideas below.

My Favorite Food, Being a Good Friend, or Staying Healthy

Step 1: Topic
Step 2: Ideas
Step 3: Topic Sentence
Step 4: Support Sentences
Step 5: Write Paragraph

90

Writing Paragraphs

Number each phrase below:
1 if the phrase tells who Mr. Mahooney is.
2 if it tells what he did.
3 if it tells why he did it.

<u>1</u> funny, old man

<u>3</u> because he had no home

<u>1</u> patched, colorful coat

<u>2</u> walked through the park

<u>2</u> talked and laughed with children

<u>1</u> big smile

<u>2</u> sat on bench

<u>1</u> bright blue eyes

<u>3</u> because he had no children

<u>2</u> fed birds

<u>3</u> because he enjoyed the park

<u>3</u> because he enjoyed talking to others

Use **Possible paragraphs** raphs about Mr. Mahooney. Write one paragraph for each number. Continue writing on another page if necessary.

Mr. Mahooney is a funny, old man with a big smile and bright blue eyes. He has a patched, colorful coat.

Mr. Mahooney walked through the park. He sat on a bench and fed the birds. He talked and laughed with children playing there.

Mr. Mahooney would go to the park because he had no home and no children. He enjoyed the park, and he also enjoyed talking to others.

91

Proofreading Practice:
Paragraphs

As you read the report below, you will notice that the report has not been divided into paragraphs. Read the sentences carefully. Use the proofreader's mark (¶) beside each sentence that starts a new paragraph. (Hint: There sould be four paragraphs in this report.)

Australia

¶Australia is unique because it is the only country that is also a continent. It is often called the "Land Down Under" because it lies solely in the Southern Hemisphere.¶The first settlements in Australia by the British government were made in 1788, using British prisoners. Great Britain had lost the War of Independence in the U.S. and had to find a new place to send the convicts from its overcrowded jails. Therefore, the prisoners were sent to this island country to serve their sentences. The warm, dry climate and an abundance of good grazing land soon attracted other settlers.¶Australia has a number of unusual animals. Along with about 700 species of birds and about 140 species of snakes, Australia has the world's only black swans, the koala, the kangaroo, the platypus, and the wombat. ¶Australia is divided into six states. Its capital is Canberra. Some of Australia's larger cities are Sydney, Brisbane, Adelaide, and Melbourne.

92

Proofreading Practice:
Paragraphs

As you read the report below, you will notice that the report has not been divided into paragraphs. Read the sentences carefully. Use the proofreader's mark (¶) beside each sentence that starts a new paragraph. (Hint: There sould be four paragraphs in this report.)

Olympic Games

¶The Olympic Games attract the best athletes from almost every country in the world to compete in a series of events. The modern Olympics were organized to promote the ideal of a "sound mind in a sound body" and to encourage world peace and friendship among nations.¶The five interlocking rings of the Olympic symbol represent the continents of Asia, Africa, Australia, Europe, and North and South America. At least one of the five colors of the rings is included in the flag of every nation.¶The Olympic Games are separated into the Summer Games and the Winter Games. A major city always hosts the Summer Games, while the Winter Games are always held at a winter resort.¶The Summer and Winter Games take place on a four-year cycle, two years apart. For example, the Winter Games are scheduled for 2002, and every four years after that. The Summer Games are scheduled for the year 2004, and every four years thereafter.

93

Comparison Paragraph

Often it is important to compare two or more things. In a **comparison paragraph** you will write about how the things are alike and different. You can compare people, places, things or ideas.

Before writing it may be helpful to brainstorm.
Example: Comparing cars and buses

Likenesses	Differences
Both are vehicles.	Buses are much larger.
Both carry people.	Fewer people ride in cars at
Both travel on streets.	one time.
Both have engines, motors,	People pay fares to ride buses.
bodies, wheels, etc.	Cars are owned by people.
Both run on fuel.	

Use these ideas to write two paragraphs to compare cars and buses. The topic sentences are already written for you. Write one paragraph about likenesses and one about differences. *Suggested answers given.*

Cars and buses may have more in common than you might think. Both are vehicles that travel on streets and run on fuel. Both carry people. Cars and buses have engines, motors, bodies, and wheels.

Although cars and buses are alike in many ways, there are still many differences between them. Buses are much larger than cars. Fewer people ride in cars at one time. People pay fares to ride buses. Cars, but not buses, are owned by people.

Compare: **TV** and **movies**
Brainstorm:

	Likenesses	Differences

Answers will vary.

94

Definition Paragraph

- Sometimes you may write a paragraph to define something. A **definition paragraph** tells exactly what something is, without sounding like a dictionary.

   Example: An *opera* is a play in which the actors sing their lines. An opera can tell a story about any subject. The music is written to help express the feelings of the story. Together, the words and music make opera a wonderful experience!

- It is easier to describe a thing than a feeling or attitude. These descriptions are much more personal.

   Example: *Confidence* is a feeling of being sure about something or someone. I feel confident in myself when I do well at school. I feel confident about my family and friends because I know that I count on them for their help and friendship.

Use these guidelines to write a paragraph to define each word.
Ask yourself: 1. What does it look like? or…How does it feel?
2. What does it do?
3. How does it affect me? or…How is it used?

A backpack is _____

_____

A rainbow is _____

_____

A TV commercial _____

_____

Happiness is _____

_____

Paragraphs will vary.

95

Descriptive Paragraph

- A **descriptive paragraph** tells about something that is observed or experienced. A good description makes a word picture for the reader.

   Example: The banana split was an ice cream lover's dream come true. A large, blue, oval dish was lined with long slices of bananas. On the bananas were three huge scoops of ice cream: chocolate fudge, vanilla, and strawberry. Drizzled over the vanilla scoop was loads of hot fudge sauce. Butterscotch sauce was dripping down the other two scoops. And lastly, chopped nuts were sprinkled over the sauce, with a puff of whipped cream and a cherry to top it off!

Read each topic below.
My Favorite Outfit   My Best Friend   Riding a Skateboard
My Pet   Riding a Roller Coaster   My Favorite Outdoor Place

Choose two topics. Make a list of details that could describe each one.

Topic 1. _____   **Topic 2.** _____
_____   _____
_____   _____
_____   _____

Write a topic sentence _____ details from each list to
write suppo_____ tive paragraph.

Answers will vary.

topic sentence
_____
_____
_____
_____
_____

96

Explanatory Paragraph

- An **explanatory paragraph** tells how to do something.

   Example: cook spaghetti, build treehouse, wash car, study for test

Use the plan below to write an explanatory paragraph. Before writing your paragraph, organize your ideas below.

Topic: _____

I. What materials are needed? _____

_____

II. What is the step-by-step plan? (in order) _____

_____

III. What are the final result_____

_____

Answers will vary.

1. Choose a top__
2. Write a topic sentence that tells what will be explained.
3. Write a sentence that tells what materials are needed.
4. Write sentences that give steps in the correct order (Remember to use "time" and "sequence" words. Example: today, tomorrow, first, last).
5. Write sentences to give special details.
6. Conclude with sentence that tells the final results.

         How to _____

_____
_____
_____
_____

97

Expository Paragraph

- An **expository paragraph** gives detailed information, either facts or opinions or both.

   Example: My favorite sport is swimming. It not only is fun and refreshing on a hotday, but it is also a great way to exercise. I go swimming almost every day in the summer.

Write an expository paragraph on each subject to tell…

All About Me

My favorite pastime is _____

_____

I think my family is super because _____

_____

Summer is important to me because _____

Answers will vary.

When I grow _____

_____

If I could be anywhere in the world, _____

_____

My favorite way to spend a Saturday afternoon _____

_____
_____
_____

98

Persuasive Paragraph

- You probably have strong opinions about many subjects. A **persuasive paragraph** is a way to express strong opinions and to try to make others feel the same way. You may have strong feelings about current events, clothes, homework, chores, TV shows, pollution, or many other topics.

Think of a topic that you feel strongly about in a positive way, and a topic you feel strongly about in a negative way.

Follow these steps to write a persuasive paragraph about each topic.
1. Choose a topic.
2. Write a topic sentence that states your strong opinion and why you feel this way.
3. Write several supportive sentences that give your reasons. Try to include several facts as well as feelings.
4. End with a sentence that summarizes your strong opinion.

I. Topic_____ (Positive opinion)

_____

Answers will vary.

II. Topic_____ (Negative opinion)

99

Writing About Pictures in Sequence

Do you ever read comic books? Comic book picture stories are drawn in a special order. That special order is called **sequence**. Sequence tells what comes first, next, and last.

The pictures below are drawn in sequence. They tell part of a picture story. Think about what the pictures show. Then draw a picture in the last space to complete the story.

First   Next   Last

Now write three sentences that describe the pictures of the girl. Be sure to write your sentences in sequence.

First _____

Next _____

Pictures and sentences will vary.

Last _____

100

Writing About Pictures in Sequence

The pictures below are not in sequence. Put the pictures in sequence so that they show a story. Write first, next, or last under each correct picture.

_____last_____   _____first_____   _____next_____

Now write three sentences that describe the picture story above.

First _____

Next _____

Sentences will vary.

Last _____

Write On Your Own

On another sheet of paper, draw a picture story of your own. Use three or more pictures for your story. Then, under each picture, write a sentence that describes it. Be sure your pictures and sentences are in sequence. You may use one of the ideas below, or you may think up your own idea.
- Flying a Plane
- Making a Pizza
- Scoring a Point in a Game

101

Writing with Sequence Words

Look at the pictures.

Before   After

Certain words always tell sequence. They are called **sequence words**. *Before* and *after* are sequence words. Some other sequence words are *first*, *then*, *next*, *last*, and *finally*.

Read the next paragraph. Then underline the sequence words in it.

> Mel looked at the painting, <u>first</u> with his head tilted to the left, <u>then</u> with it tilted to the right. <u>Next</u> he tried squinting at the painting. <u>Finally</u> he decided the painting was okay if you liked smashed fruit.

102

Writing with Sequence Words

The following paragraph uses sequence words. But the sequence of events is backwards. Rewrite the paragraph on the lines below by starting with the first event and ending with the last event. Change the sequence words so that they tell the correct order.

The elegant Lester LeMouche strolled down the avenue to his favorite restaurant. Before that, he splashed aftershave on his jaw and threaded a rosebud through the buttonhole in his jacket. And before that, he got dressed. Earlier he showered and shaved. At first, he peered at his pocket watch

Suggested answer given.

First, Lester LeMouche peered at his pocket watch and saw that it was dinner time. Then he showered and shaved. Next, he got dressed. After that, he splashed aftershave on his jaw and threaded a rosebud through the buttonhole in his jacket. Finally, the elegant Lester LeMouche strolled down the avenue to his favorite restaurant.

Write On Your Own

On another piece of paper, write a paragraph about your future. Tell about your plans. Write about what you might be doing two years from now, five years from now, and ten years from now. Use sequence words and circle each sequence word that you use.

103

Writing About Activities in Sequence

Are you one of those people who find it hard to get organized in the morning? Or do you follow a certain sequence?

Here are some things most people do every morning. On the lines below, write them in a sequence that makes sense.

eat breakfast	put on a coat
turn off the alarm	get out of bed
get dressed	brush your teeth

Suggested answers given.

First, I turn off the alarm.

Second, I get out of bed.

Third, I get dressed.

Fourth, I eat breakfast.

Fifth, I brush my teeth.

Last, I put on a coat.

104

Writing About Activities in Sequence

Imagine that while you're walking on the beach you see a bottle washed ashore. It has a message inside. What's the message? Write it on the line.

Now think about where the bottle came from. Did it come from a boat, a desert island, a faraway land — or from your friend who likes to play jokes?

Write a paragraph about how the bottle got to the beach. Tell who wrote the message and when. Tell some details about the bottle's journey. Be sure your sentences are in sequence.

Answers will vary.

Write On Your Own

What is your favorite game? How do you play it? On another sheet of paper, write a paragraph about the game using sequence words to describe how it is played.

105

Combining Sentences

- Combining sentence parts when you revise your writing can make a sentence smooth and can cut out extra words as well.
  Babe is a video I really like. *Pinocchio* is good, too. *Matilda* is one of my favorites.
  Babe, Pinocchio, and *Matilda* are three of my favorite videos or I really like *Babe, Pinocchio,* and *Matilda.*

Practice

You do not need all the words in the following sentences to say what you want to say.
Rewr *Possible answers given.* e to make one well-combined sentence.

1. I loved *James and the Giant Peach* by Roald Dahl. I also loved *Matilda* by Dahl.
   I loved *James and the Giant Peach* and *Matilda* by Roald Dahl.

2. *Oink* was illustrated by Arthur Geisert. Geisert illustrated *Haystack*, too.
   Oink and *Haystack* were illustrated by Arthur Geisert.

3. *Jumanji* is a really weird story. *Bad Day at Riverbend* is strange, too.
   Both *Jumanji* and *Bad Day at Riverbend* are weird stories.

4. *The Book of Hot Lists for Kids* gave me some great ideas for things to do. *The Kids' Summer Handbook* taught me some things, too.
   Both *The Book of Hot Lists for Kids* and *The Kids' Summer Handbook* gave me ideas for things to do.

5. Books make my weekends fun. CDs also give me some fun things to do.
   Books and CDs make my weekends fun.

106

Combining Sentences

- If you are saying two things about the same person or place, you can often combine these parts into one sentence. Do this by using more than one verb in a sentence.

    Our class **planted** a garden. We **weeded** the garden, too.

    Our class **planted and weeded** the garden.

    We **found** a video about crops the Inca planted. We **watched** the video.

    We **found and watched** a video about crops the Inca planted.

Practice

Combine each pair of sentences into one sentence that has two verbs. Write the new sentence on the line.

1. Nancy Ward thought about her Cherokee people. She worried about them.

    Nancy Ward thought and worried about her Cherokee people.

2. Nancy talked to the leaders. She begged them to listen to her.

    Nancy talked to the leaders and begged them to listen to her.

3. She led her people. She showed them a way to survive.

    She led her people and showed them a way to survive.

4. Nancy also talked to the white people. She showed them how they could have peace.

    Nancy also talked to the white people and showed them how they could have peace.

107

Combining Sentences

- You can improve a piece of writing by using one exact word in place of a whole sentence.

    The parrot has beautiful feathers. They are very **colorful**.

    The parrot has beautiful, **colorful** feathers.

    Bats eat mosquitoes and other insects. Bats are **useful** creatures.

    Useful bats eat mosquitoes and other insects or Bats are **useful** because they eat mosquitoes and other insects.

Practice

Combine the sentences in each pair. Write a new sentence by adding a single word from one sentence to the other.   Suggested answers given.

1. My aunt doesn't like this winter weather. It's cold almost every day.

    My aunt doesn't like this winter weather when it's cold almost every day.

2. She often wears unusual winter clothes. She wears colorful winter clothes.

    She often wears colorful, unusual winter clothes.

3. On really cold days, she wears a fluffy jacket. The jacket is purple.

    On really cold days, she wears a fluffy, purple jacket.

4. She also wears a cap with a pom-pom on top. The cap is made of wool.

    She also wears a wool cap with a pom-pom on top.

5. She says she likes her winter clothes. They are warm.

    She says she likes her warm winter clothes.

108

Combining Sentences

- You can combine sentences by using a phrase in place of a wordy sentence. A **phrase** is a group of related words that does not have a subject or verb.

    My friend taught me step dancing. She grew up in Ireland.

    My friend **from Ireland** taught me step dancing.

    That man enjoys watching the dancers. He uses a cane.

    That man **with the cane** enjoys watching the dancers.

Practice

Change one sentence into a phrase and place it in the other sentence. Write the new sentence on the line.

1. We watched our neighbor walk by. She led a beautiful dog.

    We watched our neighbor walk by with a beautiful dog.

2. Our neighbor seems friendly. Her house is that brick one.

    Our neighbor in that brick house seems friendly.

3. The Newfoundland puppy is hers, too! It has a floppy ear.

    The Newfoundland puppy with the floppy ear is hers, too.

4. She and the dog are going on a hike. She wants to reach Crater Lake.

    She and the dog are going on a hike to Crater Lake.

5. She walks the dog every day. The dog wears a leash.

    She walks the dog on a leash every day.

109

Combining Sentences

- You can combine two sentences with these words: **and**, **but**, and **or**. The two parts of the combined sentence are separated by a comma.

    Many people drive to work, **but** people in cities often use public transportation.

    Cars pollute the air, **and** gas for a car may be expensive.

    You can choose to fly long distances, **or** you can drive for several days.

Practice

Combine these pairs of sentences using **and**, **but**, or **or**. Write the new sentence on the line. Be sure to add a comma.

1. Trains have crossed the United States since the 1860s. They have moved millions of people.

    Trains have crossed the United States since the 1860's, and they have moved millions of people.

2. Today many people still love to ride the train. Many others think it is too slow.

    Today many people still love to ride the train, but many others think it is too slow.

3. Many families think driving is the easiest for them. It can be tiring.

    Many families think driving is the easiest for them, but it can be tiring.

4. Many people with babies choose to drive. They can fly faster.

    Many people with babies choose to drive, or they can fly faster.

110

Combining Sentences
Practice

Practice combining sentences below.

1. The quarter rolled under the sofa.
   The dime rolled under the sofa.
   The quarter and dime rolled under the sofa.

2. The fourth graders are in the school play.
   The fifth graders are in the school play.
   The fourth and fifth graders are in the school play.

3. The kids went to the library.
   The kids checked out books.
   The kids went to the library and checked out books.

4. The sandwiches are in our picnic basket.
   The chips are in our picnic basket.
   The sandwiches and chips are in our picnic basket.

5. Katy folded her camp clothes.
   Katy packed them in her luggage.
   Katy folded her camp clothes and packed them in her luggage.

6. Mom came to my school's Open House.
   Dad came to my school's Open House.
   Mom and Dad came to my school's Open House.

7. All the guests ate refreshments.
   All the guests had a great time.
   All guests ate refreshments and had a great time.

8. Our teacher gave us a math assignment.
   Our teacher told us to work quietly.
   Our teacher gave us a math assignment and told us to work quietly.

111

Combining Sentences

When sentences are short and choppy, they can be combined into one good sentence. Combine each group of sentences below into one sentence. The first one is done for you.

Suggested answers given.

1. Three children played ball. They jumped rope. They were happy.
   Three happy children played ball and jumped rope.

2. These marbles are bright. They are shiny. They are mine.
   These bright, shiny marbles are mine.

3. The movie was long. It was funny. I liked it.
   I liked the long, funny movie.

4. Those are fishing boats. They are old. They sail out on the ocean.
   Those old fishing boats sail out on the ocean.

5. The day is windy. The day is cloudy. It is rainy.
   The day is windy, cloudy, and rainy.

6. The purse was black. It was stolen. It was not found.
   The black purse was stolen and not found.

7. Lee's dog has a red collar. He is lost. He is black.
   Lee's lost black dog has a red collar.

8. The window is dirty. It is broken. It is stuck.
   The window is dirty, stuck, and broken.

112

Combining Sentences

Two sentences can be written as one sentence by using connecting words. Read the two sentences. Choose one of the words to the left to combine the two sentences into one sentence.

1. We can eat now. We can eat after the game.

   while
   or
   because
   We can eat now, or we can eat after the game.

2. We stood on the cabin's deck. The sun rose over the deck.

   as
   or
   but
   We stood on the cabin's deck as the sun rose over the deck.

3. Sarah wanted to watch TV. She had lots of homework to finish.

   because
   when
   but
   Sarah wanted to watch TV, but she had lots of homework to finish.

4. The concert did not begin on time. The conductor was late arriving.

   until
   because
   while
   The concert did not begin on time, because the conductor was late arriving.

5. The spectators cheered and applauded. The acrobats completed their performances.

   when
   if
   but
   The spectators cheered and applauded when the acrobats completed their performances.

6. The baseball teams waited in their dugouts. The rain ended and the field was uncovered.

   or
   until
   after
   The baseball teams waited in their dugouts until the rain ended and the field was uncovered.

113

Friendly Letter

A **friendly letter** is a casual letter between family or friends. A friendly letter can express your own personality. It can be written for a special reason or just for fun.

Write a friendly letter to a "friend" in another city. Invite the friend to visit you some time during the summer. Follow these guidelines:
   A. Heading: Write your address and date. (your street name and number on the first line; your city, state abbreviation and zip code on the second line)
   B. Greeting: (**Example:** Dear (Fill in name of person to whom you are writing.))
   C. Body: Write three paragraphs.
      First: pleasant greeting and invitation
      Second: details about visit
      Third: summarize excitement about visit
   D. Closing (**Example:** Your friend)
   E. Signature (your name)

Answers will vary.

114

Business Letter

Read the letter below. Notice the spacing and form of the letter. Notice also the names of the parts of the letter.

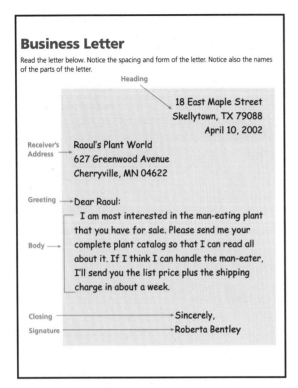

Heading

18 East Maple Street
Skellytown, TX 79088
April 10, 2002

Receiver's Address

Raoul's Plant World
627 Greenwood Avenue
Cherryville, MN 04622

Greeting

Dear Raoul:

Body

I am most interested in the man-eating plant that you have for sale. Please send me your complete plant catalog so that I can read all about it. If I think I can handle the man-eater, I'll send you the list price plus the shipping charge in about a week.

Closing

Sincerely,

Signature

Roberta Bentley

115

Business Letter

Write answers to the following questions based on the letter on page 115.

1. Besides trouble, what is Roberta Bentley asking for?
   a plant catalog

2. Where is the receiver's address written — on the right or the left side of the page?
   left

3. What two things are included in the heading?
   address and date

4. What is the closing?
   Sincerely

5. What is the greeting?
   Dear Raoul

6. What punctuation mark follows the greeting?
   colon

7. In what part of the letter is the purpose expressed?
   body

Write On Your Own

Pretend you have one million dollars. Using another sheet of paper, write a business letter that orders something or many things that you want. Or you may decide to give the money away. In that case write your letter to someone you would like to receive your generous gift. Follow the form of the business letter on page 115.

116

Proofreading Practice:
Addressing Envelopes

Now that you have learned how to write a letter, you need to learn how to address an envelope. In the upper right corner of the envelope, write your name. Below your name, write your street address followed on the next line by your city, state, and Zip code. In the center of the envelope, write the name of the person to whom you are writing. On the line below the person's name, write that person's street address followed by the person's city, state, and Zip code. Remember to capitalize the names of people and places. Also notice the comma placed between the city and state.

Dr. B. J. Morris
Granville Hospital
1814 Riverside Street
Columbus, OH 43206

Ford Motor Company
201 Henry Ford Drive
Detroit, MI 62805

Look at the envelope below. Correct the capitalization and punctuation. Use the envelope above to help you.

megan cullen
275 daisy lane
boston ma 02101

mr. timothy parlette
917 south market
las vegas nv 89109

117

Writing an Invitation

An invitation must give all the necessary information. It must at least answer the questions **who**, **what**, **when**, and **where**.

Write an invitation using the information below.
WHO: (person you are inviting)
      (your name)
WHAT: A surprise party
WHEN: Saturday, March 12, at 2:00 p.m.
WHERE: 1112 Circle Drive

Suggested answers given.

To: Mary

You are invited to a surprise birthday party for Susie on Saturday, March 12 at 2:00 p.m. My address is 1112 Circle Drive.

From: Kathy

118

NOTES

NOTES

NOTES

NOTES